The Me1st Method

Hands-On Leadership Development *for* New Roles *and* Big Challenges

Mike Palanski, Ph.D.

The Me1st Method

Hands-On Leadership Development for New Roles and Big Challenges

ISBNs

Paperback: 979-8-9858294-0-2

Audiobook 979-8-9858294-1-9

EPUB:-979-8-9858294-2-6

To my Executive MBA students (especially those from early in my career):

These are the ideas I would have liked to share with you during our time together. But I did not yet know them fully, and I would not have been able to develop them without your trust and patience. Whatever small wisdom I imparted to you, you have already repaid me a thousand times.

"Growth is this: to be defeated by ever greater things."
–Rainer Maria Rilke

CONTENTS

Foreword   9
Introduction   13

Part I   19

1. The Mystery of Focusing on Self First   21
2. The Next Big Challenge   28
3. Overcoming the Three Big Hurdles Faced by Next Big
   Challenge Leaders   37
4. The Seductive Trap of the Quick-Fix   51

Part II   59

5. The Science of Leader Development   61
6. Finding the Next Big Challenge: Motivate   76
7. From Finding to Facing the Next Big Challenge: Educate
   & Evaluate   93
8. A Plan for Facing the Next Big Challenge: Strategize   115
9. Facing and Embracing the Next Big Challenge: Test   125
10. Structured Support for The Me1st Method – and Why
    You Need It   135

Part III   149

11. Creating Your Personal Leadership Purpose Statement   151
12. Creating a Team Charter   160
13. Creating an Organizational Change Manifesto   171
14. You Got This   185

Acknowledgments   189
Notes   191
About the Author   195
Before You Go   197

FOREWORD

I started working with Mike in 2009 as a newly minted Ph.D. in my first real academic job. I was working at the University of Limerick and was introduced to Mike through a mutual connection. We began our first research project together–a painfully fascinating "historiometric analysis" aimed at discovering how Nobel Prize winners tapped their creative genius. I could tell right away he had a sharp mind, strong drive, big ideas, clever wit, and a compassionate heart. On those early phone calls I didn't, however, picture him bald. It wasn't until years later when I first met Mike—in person—in 2012 when he showed up at my house with his family to do some laundry on a trip abroad. To his defense, I had offered what I believed weary travelers with small kids need most: a hot meal and clean socks. We—and our families—became instant friends.

Since our Nobel Prize study, we have written and re-written dozens of papers together (10 published in journals and edited volumes and others in the pipeline). He is simply an exceptional co-author and collaborator. He is an expert in the field of leadership, leadership development, and ethics and has received international recognition for this work. He has published in the absolute top journals such as the *Academy of Management Review*, *The Leadership Quarterly*, and *Journal of Business Ethics*. His work is well-cited and he is one of the "go-to" experts on "whole-person" or multi-domain leadership and behavioral integrity. What separates this book and program from so many others on the market is the research behind it. The **Me1st Method** is a beautifully accessible translation of decades of research into a practical method.

The heart of much of our research together is on leader identity--the relatively simple idea that the "being" of leadership is as important (or perhaps more) than the "doing." With a quick search, you'll find hundreds of books professing "5 simple rules," "three essential skills," or even "21 irrefutable laws" you must follow to be a good leader. Although there may be some great insights, most of these books are built on a formula that worked for the authors in their unique contexts and relationships, with no guarantee it will work for you in your unique situations. No one situation or relationship or project requires the same exact leadership, so a simple "formula" just can't work for everyone across the board. What makes an identity-based approach different is that it focuses on the single constant across all leadership situations you will face—you! It empowers you to be the agent of change in these relationship systems.

In addition to Mike's development of ideas, I have a unique ability to speak to Mike's development of people. Research collaborations across universities are frequent—collaborations that also extend into teaching and consulting are rare. We have been involved with joint student learning projects, shared development tools and methods, and co-facilitated our first major consulting projects. Many of these projects were Mike's ideas and I was lucky to be involved in them. Over the years we have brainstormed and experimented extensively to promote student engagement and to help burgeoning leaders work through challenges. We have worked one-on-one with leaders and presented to small groups and large groups. Over the years, we've made many changes and have learned so much about how to best help others, but through our discussions and work with others his desire to help others grow was at the heart.

To that end, I owe a lot of my own career success to promptings from Mike. My first experience with a 360 survey was when Mike coached me. I still remember the insight around needing to balance an individualized consideration of where people were at with an ability to draw the best from them. It's the same paradox many women leaders face: the need to be demanding and caring; to be approachable and maintain appropriate boundaries; to be assertive and participative. The 360 helped me see I was facing the same challenges with my colleagues, clients, students, and kids. Defaulting to "nice" left me both feeling like a "pushover" and largely ineffective at bringing out the best in others. Further, it wasn't allowing me to best live out my core value of development. Through reflection, experimentation, and feedback, I've improved to embrace the "both/and " rather than the "either/or" in these leadership paradoxes. I think you will find Mike's mastered that paradox: he is appropriately supportive and challenging.

Informally, Mike has prompted me to find, coached me to face, and encouraged me to embrace numerous "Big Challenges" in my professional and personal life—from projects that stretched me beyond my comfort zone to an international move, from self-advocating to embracing parenting challenges. Mike has prompted me to ask myself the big questions, to take one step at a time, to reflect, to experiment, and ultimately to grow. If you're up for it, I have no doubt he will do the same for you! Enjoy the journey!

–DR. MICHELLE HAMMOND, OAKLAND UNIVERSITY

INTRODUCTION

Hello. My name is Mike Palanski, and I collaborate with professionals like you to develop keen insights and create meaningful change. It's what I love to do - as a professor, a coach, a speaker, and a writer. My primary expertise is in leadership development, and I especially enjoy working with leaders who are changing roles and taking on big challenges.

If you are a leader who is taking on a new position, moving to a new company, switching to a new career, or (perhaps most daunting of all) staying right where you are—same role, same team, same title—but attempting to do something important that you've never done before, then there's a special designation for you.

You are a **Next Big Challenge** leader.

Next Big Challenge leaders include:

- The accomplished individual contributor who joins an Executive MBA program to learn about the big picture of business in order to be promoted
- The bank branch manager who was recently promoted to regional manager and is learning how to stay out of the day-to-day details in order to grow the business
- The stay-at-home parent who has years of experience leading volunteers and is now getting ready to restart a professional career
- The wildly successful corporate trainer who feels called to something greater and is contemplating the possibility of starting their own consultancy
- The not-for-profit executive director who desires to create a truly lasting impact

Now, here's the cool thing about being a Next Big Challenge leader: just like how every great story is built on three acts (the setup, the conflict, and the resolution), taking on big challenges has its own natural process, its own predictable flow. This flow is about finding, facing, and embracing your Next Big Challenge.

And, you know what is even cooler? The key to this process is to focus on yourself first. It might sound a bit counter-intuitive, I know - but a good deal of evidence-based research supports this notion. The purpose of this book is to make that research vivid and useful for leaders like you. I call this hands-on approach the **Me1st Method**.

HOW TO READ THIS BOOK

I wrote this book to share what I know and help you develop insights and obtain results before you even finish reading. Leadership has been my professional life for almost two decades. I've learned a lot, and I want to put it out into the world with the confidence that it will do some good.

I want to help you create keen insights and meaningful change (for yourself, your team, and your organization) by taking the somewhat unusual approach of focusing on yourself. That is why I wrote this book, coach Next Big Challenge leaders, and do original research. It's how I teach my classes and speak to different audiences. This desire is at the very heart of who I am and all I do as a professional.

To do these things, I have structured the book in this way:

First, we are going to consider what leadership looks like when you lead yourself first. Next, we are going to talk about what being a Next Big Challenge leader is like by taking a look at a few stories of actual leaders, the challenges they found themselves facing, and what they did to keep moving forward. Then we are going to look at some of the biggest hurdles that Next Big Challenge leaders face (teaser: they are formidable but also predictable, and therefore overcome-able).

After that, we will nerd out on the science behind the **Me1st Method**; in other words, the research behind all of this stuff. And then we will look at the main attraction: the step-by-step **Me1st Method** of developing Next Big Challenge leaders:

- **M**otivate (finding and defining your Next Big Challenge)
- **E**ducate & **E**valuate (developing your leadership knowledge/skills and assessing your current situation)
- **1** thing at a time (not a step, really—just a little reminder)
- **S**trategize (get your plan in place)
- **T**est (experiment and embrace the Next Big Challenge)

We will look at why Next Big Challenge leaders need support (and the types of support you need). And finally, I will help you get started by walking you through the process of creating your Personal Leadership Purpose Statement. I'll also guide you to create a Team Charter and an Organizational Change Manifesto. By the time you are finished with this book, you will have the tools you need to find, face, and embrace your Next Big Challenge by following the **Me1st Method**.

Before we go any further, I do want to make one thing clear: Me1st is exactly what it says:

me, first

But it's not:

- me, alone
- me, to the exclusion of all others
- me, and others' interests be damned
- me, Me, ME! ALL ABOUT ME!

We are not trying to create an army of narcissistic leaders here. Instead, what I want to do is to help you to define yourself so well as a leader that you can show up to any situation with your own sense of self intact. You can present your own best thinking and display emotional maturity, while remaining connected to others.

THIS BOOK IN A NUTSHELL

The entirety of this book can be summed up in three points:

1. Finding, facing, and embracing the Next Big Challenge requires hard work for leaders
2. This work is best accomplished by following the **Me1st Method**

3. This work is easier and faster with collaborative support and
   guidance

Along the way, I hope you get to know me a bit better. You'll see my
nerdy professor side, my passion for developing leaders, and
sometimes my dry sense of humor at its dad-joke best. I even cuss a
little at times. But more than anything else, here's what I want you to
know about me:

I've been a high achiever all of my life, with a real knack for being able
to read people and adapt to them in a likable and affable way. These
qualities have served me very well (and in many ways, continue to do
so). But something was missing. I knew I wasn't at my highest
potential. Until I learned that taking a Me1st approach is not selfish at
all (in fact, as I'll argue later in the book, I think it is actually the key
to real service and love of others), I wasn't able to face my own Next
Big Challenge(s) and become what I believed I could be—as a
professor, as a coach, as a business person, or as a dad, a husband, or a
friend.

In different ways, I have seen this breakthrough story play out again
and again in my work with my clients and students. You will meet
some of them in Chapter 1.

So even if you stop reading right here (but please don't!), I want you
to walk away with this one idea:

Following the **Me1st Method** is the best way to find, face, and
embrace the Next Big Challenge—to create keen insights and
meaningful change for yourself, your team, and your organization.

To help you do that, I'm putting my best thinking forward in this
book. I try to use a variety of examples and ideas in the hopes that you

see yourself in these pages. But let me also extend two additional helps to you:

1. Whether you purchased this book or received it as a gift, you are entitled to some valuable complimentary bonus content just for being a reader, including:

- A 60-page companion workbook
- A self-guided video course to creating your Personal Leadership Purpose Statement

2. If what you read in these pages resonates and you desire more help, I would like to explore the possibility of collaborating with you as one of my coaching clients.

To learn more please visit:

Me1stMethod.com

As we say in my hometown of Pittsburgh: that's it, Fort Pitt.

Happy reading!

Mike

Part I:

Why Leaders Who Are Looking to
Find, Face, and Embrace the Next Big Challenge
Should Be Thinking **Me1st**

1

THE MYSTERY OF FOCUSING ON SELF FIRST

"If you think taking care of yourself is selfish, change your mind. If you don't, you're simply ducking your responsibilities."—ANN RICHARDS

Think of the leaders that you admire most. What is it about those people that make them so effective, so admirable? My guess is that the qualities that you are thinking about go beyond the noticeable characteristics of the person—their physical description, their demographic characteristics, or even their charisma. These qualities go beyond the things they do—the goals they achieve, the people they inspire.

In my experience, the leaders we admire have unique characteristics and do good things, but there is something more. It's almost like they have a unique way of being in the world, isn't it?

- They enjoy great freedom and refuse to be tied to petty policies or people, but they also have impressive self-discipline

- They are strong individuals who are unafraid to stand alone, but they never lose connections with others (even when they disagree)
- They have a wealth of wisdom, but they don't lord it over others
- They seem to see further than most, but they never lose sight of the present moment
- They seem to consider everyone's interests and be on everyone's side, including their own

As a university professor and researcher in the field of leadership, I have spent the last 17+ years studying effective leadership. Even after all that time, I am no less fascinated by leadership than the day I walked into my first seminar as a brand-new PhD student. I suppose it is because there truly is no magic formula, no silver bullet, and no one-size-fits-all solution.

But if there is one defining characteristic of effective leaders, it is this: **they view leadership as a life-long practice**. As such, the primary focus of that practice is... **themselves**. In other words, the best leaders focus on themselves *at least as much* as they focus on other people or circumstances.

That might sound crazy, I know. In many ways, it goes against the conventional wisdom about servant leadership, putting others first, leaders eating last, thinking less of yourself, inspiring others, doing great things, and so on. But I think the notion that focusing on self really is the most effective way for leaders to develop.

Before we go any further, you need to know something about me: I am not in the business of convincing. I mean, you're a grown-ass adult. You can read critically and do your own thinking. So, I am not going to coax you into using the **Me1st Method**, but I do want to lay out a reasonable case for it. I want to show you the science behind it and how it all works. But first, let me show you what it can be like to focus on yourself first. (Please note that names and non-essential details are altered to protect client confidentiality.)

FACING THE NEXT BIG CHALLENGE: MEET NANCY

Nancy was an extraordinary nurse and had enjoyed a great deal of early-career success, first as a practicing nurse and then as a charge nurse overseeing other nurses. Before she knew it, she was promoted to a nurse manager position and had direct responsibility for over 70 nurses and technicians. Nancy loved her job, her patients, and especially her staff. And they loved her, too. The problem was that Nancy was quickly becoming burned out.

By the way, do you know how resilient nurses can be? Nurses are used to pulling 12-hour shifts with barely time to take a pee or scarf down some food. They are there when people are stripped of dignity, and sometimes of life itself. Nurses are truly a unique blend of compassion, skill, and courage.

Yet there she was, racing towards exhaustion and burnout. Why? After talking about her situation at length with me, Nancy concluded that she was still attempting to do what she had always done and been good at—being there to offer support and advice to anyone that asked. That method worked fine when it was just her. It worked OK when she had only a few nurses to support, but it was about to wreck her when she was supporting 70+ other people.

Nancy had to face the critical question, 'What do I need to be able to continue to show up for others and be successful?" And face it she did.

She first determined that she needed to free up time and capacity (both mental and emotional) to focus on her own tasks. She came up with a simple but effective strategy for doing so. Nancy wrote herself a note and kept it with her at all times (usually on her clipboard). The note read:

What other options do you have to answer this question?

That's it. She started asking that question, without fail. She encouraged people to seek out their own options first but assured them that she would be available if they were truly stuck. Within a week, the number of random questions she was asked dropped significantly. She took some other actions, too, but this was the one action that turned the tide and created some margin for her.

EMBRACING THE NEXT BIG CHALLENGE: MEET SAM

Sam was extremely effective and enjoyed success as an engineer. His technical know-how and ability to deliver results set him apart from his peers. Although no one doubted his engineering expertise, his ability to lead was very much in question. He often met stiff resistance when leading projects and his desire to be promoted appeared to be in jeopardy.

When we first met, he had a good idea of what he desired to achieve. He knew what his challenge was and was ready to embrace it: to lead others. In truth, he even had a pretty good "textbook" understanding of what effective leaders do. What he didn't quite realize was that other people—those he was leading—had a completely different interpretation of his actions. What he saw as giving helpful, pointed advice that he knew would work was seen by others as insensitive micro-managing.

In Sam's case, we used a 360-degree survey to provide insight. A 360-degree survey is a leader development tool in which the leader and those that know the leader well (boss, peers, direct reports, but possibly also family and friends) answer a series of questions about the leader. The results allow the leader to compare how they see themselves vs. how others see them. The results from Sam's 360-degree survey were eye-opening. He began to realize that he needed to expand his people skills–and we worked together to do so.

Sam improved dramatically as a leader and was soon promoted into a significant managerial role. After a few years, he accepted an offer for a more impactful position with another company.

FINDING THE NEXT BIG CHALLENGE: MEET ANGELA

Angela had built a good career for herself in a traditionally male-dominated environment. She was dedicated, analytical, and had built a reputation for influencing her team and her clients with her affable and warm personality. She had a keen, intuitive sense about what people needed and wanted and was usually able to adapt to provide it to them.

When we began working together, we started with some foundational work like creating a Personal Leadership Purpose Statement (PLPS— just like you can do in Chapter 11) and completing some exercises to better understand her unique leader identity.

This is where things get interesting. After some back and forth discussion between us over the course of a few weeks, she had this insight: "I've never really taken the time to focus on myself. I've been so busy—and successful—focusing on others that I have lost my own voice. I feel like I am beginning to find it again." As a result, she began experimenting with some ideas about how to find and use her voice.

It wasn't long before she was promoted—a clear sign that she was on the right track.

FINDING, FACING, AND EMBRACING THE NEXT BIG CHALLENGE: MEET MIKE

Angela's story is a great transition to telling you a bit about my own story. I'll admit that when she found some insight about the value of focusing on herself, even I was a bit surprised by her statement. For me, Angela was one of those "Gee, how am I ever going to provide value to her?" clients because she was already rockin' it in her career.

If I had coached Angela a few years prior, I am convinced that I would have been far less valuable to her.

Why? Because in those days I was really hustling to prove my worth. As a coach. As a professor. As a husband. As a father. Really in just about in every important role I had. Although I wouldn't have admitted it, my *de facto* goal in every relationship was to be the good-natured, value-adding man. Deep down, though, I yearned for greater freedom and wisdom.

In an unexpected turn of events, **I discovered that how I *view myself* and how I *relate to myself* form the foundations for all of my other relationships**. It was at this point that I believe I truly began to be present and valuable to others. The more I became skillful at relating to myself, the more I was able to help others. **I no longer needed a particular reaction from them to be OK.** That's why I could help Angela: because I could trust the process instead of trusting my own need to be valuable.

I'm not perfect at this practice and I never will be. But I am better than I used to be and I trust that I will continue to get better by taking care of myself first. This is a life long journey.

NEXT STEPS

These examples serve to highlight the central message I am trying to convey in this book: a healthy focus on self—a **Me1st** approach—is the best path to grow as a leader in order to find, face, and embrace the Next Big Challenge. The rest of the information in this book is geared towards this singular end.

As we continue, keep these things in mind:

- In any social system (like workplace or family), our own actions are the single best point of leverage we have for influencing the system
- The relationship we have with ourselves is both the practice field and the proving ground for how we relate with others
- Working on yourself as a leader generates greater freedom, greater wisdom, and greater connectedness with others

Are you ready to keep exploring? Then let's go!

2

THE NEXT BIG CHALLENGE

"There's always a new challenge to keep you motivated" —SEAN CONNERY

I believe that all kinds of leaders in all kinds of situations can benefit from the **Me1st Method** of leader development. However, I have written this book specifically for leaders who wish to find, face, and embrace the Next Big Challenge.

If you are a leader who is considering what is next, who is in the process of actually making a change, or who—having recently made a big change—is trying to figure out what to do now, you have a special title: you are a Next Big Challenge leader. (OK, so this is a name that I made up, but I think it works pretty well).

Think about our journeys as leaders. It's a cycle of finding, facing, and embracing the Next Big Challenge. It involves a change of some sort, and the intensity of energy and focus (depicted in the outer arrows) peaks as we make that change.

Next Big Challenge Cycle

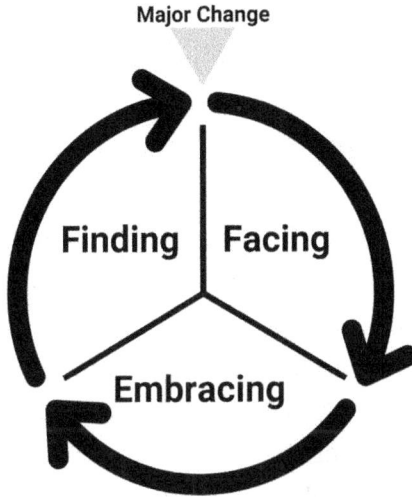

Major Change

Finding | Facing

Embracing

Starting at the bottom, there are times of relative calm, where we feel in control and everything and everyone seems to be thriving. We are not really thinking about a new challenge at all. Those times are easy and enjoyable, and we can appreciate them when they happen.

But like the words from that old Semisonic song *Closing Time*, "Every new beginning comes from some other beginning's end." This period of calm and prosperity came about from a prior challenge that you faced in the past, didn't it? In other words, you have found, faced, and eventually embraced previous challenges before, and successfully negotiated them.

At some point, we begin to feel a call towards something else: something more challenging, new, and different. Here, we are asking ourselves, "What's next?" We start trying to find our Next Big Challenge. At first it is an inkling, barely noticeable. Often it is "I don't know what I want, but it isn't what I have right now." We are now firmly in the process of **finding** our Next Big Challenge.

When the Next Big Challenge Finds You Instead

While it is true that we often search to find the Next Big Challenge, it is equally true that the Next Big Challenge sometimes finds us, isn't it?

Sometimes we are just going about life and everything seems to be just fine. Then when we see or hear or read something, we are startled by how much it resonates with us. We shrug it off, but it happens again. Like the whisper of "If you build it, they will come" from *Field of Dreams*, it becomes a small but real—intensely real—flicker. And that small flicker eventually becomes a hot flame, to the point where we can barely think about anything else. It becomes our central passion and drives us onward.

Other times, we are going through life and everything seems to be just fine. Then something shocking happens. Sometimes it's a positive surprise, like hitting the lottery. More often though, it's painful: a huge client quits, a natural disaster occurs, or a family member is diagnosed with a serious medical condition. We are thrust into a situation that we did not ask for and do not want. Nonetheless, the challenge is now upon us. We respond because we must.

If you picked up this book because your Next Big Challenge has already found you, please know that I see you.

I feel for you and with you.

As the challenge becomes clearer, our focus on it gradually increases. Our time and energy become more devoted to it. Eventually, we make a change; a transition. This change can come in several forms (sometimes overlapping):

- A new role
- A new company
- A new career
- A new project or initiative
- A new way of living

Once we make that transition, we are faced with a whole new set of challenges—some of which we anticipated, but many of which are a surprise. Basically, we are asking ourselves, "Now what?" We are now **facing** that Next Big Challenge—and damn it feels pretty daunting.

Eventually, we figure enough of it out to begin to see some results. We embrace the Next Big Challenge. It becomes a part of us—a part of our history …and we slowly return to a period of calm.

Then, it starts again…but this time it is a bigger desire. The Next Big Challenge (or maybe I should say the Next Next Big Challenge?) begins to emerge. We might think the cycle is repeating—and in a way it is. Maybe a better description is of an upward spiral, because we are moving on to greater things. Think of a Slinky™ or the circular ramp in a parking garage.

Anyway, you get the picture. Let's take a closer look at this process:

EXTERNAL CHANGE: THE AGONY AND THE ECSTASY

The major change during a period of challenge is often intense—and often ambivalent. Excitement about what might be coming is accompanied by fear of losing what once was. The exciting primary change (i.e., a new job) is often accompanied by a host of more mundane changes that will require resources and energy (e.g., moving to a new city, dealing with the impact on family, or even just getting set up with a new laptop and email).

Sometimes, that major change (depicted by a triangle in the graphic above) is more like a big-ass question mark. We know that our current situation is not sustainable, but we have no clue what is coming next —in other words, we are still finding our Next Big Challenge. Other times, the major change has occurred, but now we are realizing that was in fact the easy part. The 'lala land' of anticipation is quickly being replaced by the 'reinforced concrete' of reality—we are squarely in the midst of facing that Next Big Challenge. We eventually settle in. There's still much work to do, but our growing sense of confidence lets us know that we are ready for what's to come.

No matter the particulars of the external change, one thing is certain: finding, facing, and embracing the Next Big Challenge successfully requires courage and stamina.

INTERNAL CHANGE: THE PART WE OFTEN OVERLOOK

Every successful external change must be accompanied by an internal change. It is inevitable. The only real question is: will we recognize that we need an internal change process and thus attempt to do it well? Or will we simply be swept along by unseen forces?

What does that internal change look like? It can be a change in how we see the world: what we pay attention to, and what we perceive to be true. It can involve the people that we're hanging out with or our whole way of thinking about things. It can be a change in mindset: how we're going to go about doing things, the actions that we're going to take, and the values that we are going to put into action. It can show up as a change in the vision we have for our life, or our sense of mission (how we're going to carry out that vision). It can be a way that we are changing how we handle emotions and how we process what we're feeling. It can be a change in our knowledge or our skills—not just adding an extra skill or a piece of knowledge, but a fundamental shift. It might even involve a major shift in who we are.

In short, the internal change is going to look a bit different for each individual person. The common factor for Next Big Challenge leaders is summed up with this thought: "I know—or at least I sense—that something is different about me, or needs to become different about me, to face this challenge successfully."

WHAT HAPPENS WHEN WE DO NOT EMBRACE INTERNAL CHANGE?

When we do not recognize—and do not lean into—the fact that all external changes need to be accompanied by internal changes, we severely limit our own power. We hand over our ability to face challenges well to other people and to the situations in which we find ourselves. This often takes one of two forms:

First of all, we may find ourselves **perpetually in motion**. In other words, we are constantly shifting and jumping from one situation to another. We never quite seem to find stability. We live the same cycle over and over:

- We find ourselves dissatisfied, and then
- We transition to a new situation (new role, new job, new major project), and then
- We enjoy a honeymoon period for a while, but then
- We find that the situation isn't what we thought it would be, and then
- We find ourselves dissatisfied...

In our graphic, we always find ourselves in the zone of great intensity at the top. The easy zone of embrace is like a mirage in the desert. Perhaps a good name for this situation is **"leader in perpetual motion."**

Second, we may find ourselves **perpetually stuck** and being constantly sucked back into the easy zone of relative stability. We sometimes flirt with finding and facing a new challenge as we start to ponder "what's next?", but we quickly backslide. Our main desire is stability; no matter what happens, we fear upsetting the status quo. In fact, if we are honest, we will do just about anything we can to maintain the status quo, even if our external circumstances are primed for change. Instead of taking a stand for something, we're stifled by a lack of courage or initiative. We desire a change and a challenge, but quickly give up in order to make others happy, or at least to avoid making others upset. The cycle here is:

- We find ourselves dissatisfied, and then
- We dream about facing a challenge (new role, new job, new major project), and then
- We consider how others might react negatively, and then
- We rationalize how our current situation isn't so bad, and then
- We find ourselves dissatisfied...

In our graphic, we always find ourselves in the easy zone. The tense zone of challenge and change is our mirage in the desert. Perhaps a good name for this situation is **"leader stuck in the comfort zone."**

What I'd like to suggest is that the reason you're stuck in either one of those endless loops is the dynamic interplay between you the leader, the people you're involved with, and the situation in which you find yourself. More to the point, in both cases, **you are letting the people around you and the situation you are in dictate your actions**—and your level of success in meeting the Next Big Challenge.

If you find yourself in one of these two situations and you are satisfied being there, that's fine. That's cool. But this book is probably not going to help you.

Let me gently say to you: this book is for leaders who are motivated to find, face, and embrace the Next Big Challenge. It's for those who are asking "what's next?" or "now what?" with a desire to find answers and live them out.

MY HOPE FOR YOU

I have a heart for Next Big Challenge leaders like you. Leading through relatively calm times is difficult enough, but leading through a major challenge can be exceedingly difficult. As you read through the rest of this book, I hope you embrace three things:

1. The key to meeting a Big Challenge is keeping both the external and internal changes in mind

2. Finding, facing, and embracing the Next Big Challenge is easier and yields better results by following a process

3. Big Challenges need not be faced alone; there is support available

As you continue this journey, I ask you to consider the proposition I made in the introduction:

Following the **Me1st Method** is the best way to find, face, and embrace the Next Big Challenge—to create forward momentum and clear results for yourself, your team, and your organization.

If you are ready to do the hard work of looking inside yourself, then let's keep going.

3

OVERCOMING THE THREE BIG HURDLES FACED BY NEXT BIG CHALLENGE LEADERS

"I truly believe that we can overcome any hurdle that lies before us"
—GILLIAN ANDERSON

I n this chapter, I want to talk about the three biggest hurdles that Next Big Challenge leaders face. We are going to do so for three reasons:

1) I want you to expect them. They are predictable and very likely to occur

2) I want you to see them as indicators that you are on the right path

3) I want you to overcome them more quickly and easily by following the **Me1st Method**

As we explore these hurdles, I am going to use the language of *resistance* to describe them. This term comes from Steven Pressfield's excellent (and very funny) little book *The War of Art*.[1] By resistance, I am referring to the challenges, roadblocks, and hurdles that seem to materialize out of thin air about two seconds after we decide to start moving forward in an important endeavor (you know...like facing the Next Big Challenge). Resistance may come in different forms, but I believe that the common thread is that resistance always shows up as a bad, deceptive answer to legitimate questions and legitimate interests.

Before we begin, let me tell you a quick little story. Once upon a time, yours truly had a notion to become a pastor (yes...I know...*I know*... now stop laughing). So, I did the next logical thing: I applied (and was accepted) to seminary to begin studying for a master's degree in theology. About two days after I received my acceptance letter, I received another little gift in the mail. It was a CD with a recording from the seminary president talking about—you guessed it!—*resistance*. His message was simply, "Now that you have decided to come here, you will find a hundred reasons not to follow through. Don't let these reasons distract you. See you in the fall." (**Note to younger readers**: a CD—or compact disc—is simply an ancient, pre-internet way to share audio files.)

At the time, it felt a little sales-y—a sophisticated plea of "Don't change your mind!" But I've since recognized that it was a wise warning because resistance does show up in all worthwhile endeavors. Even though I didn't become a pastor (thank God...literally), one of the papers I wrote for an ethics class in seminary eventually became the basis for my doctoral dissertation in leadership. Had I given in to the resistance and not gone to seminary, who knows what path I would have taken?

Let's take a little tour of the resistance neighborhood for Next Big Challenge leaders. For each type of resistance, we will name the legitimate question or concern for leaders, and then call out the form(s) of resistance associated with each. We will also show how the **Me1st Method** is the best tool to cut that resistance down to size.

Ready? OK—here's the 411 on resistance. The skinny. The poop. The tea. The low down.

HURDLE #1: RESISTANCE FROM YOURSELF

So, here's a bad news/good news piece of insight: for most of us, the single biggest hurdle we will face is...ourselves.

Bad news? Yes, because c'mon, man! Is there anything more frustrating than tripping over our own feet? And yet, it's our own internal dialogue that often holds us back. It's how we make sense of our past experiences that impedes us. Look in the mirror, my friend. Behold! Before you lies a veritable nuclear generator of resistance.

Good news? Yes, because we can start to work on overcoming this hurdle without even getting up out of our chairs! Chopping self-imposed hurdles down to size is not easy, but at least we have immediate access to the hurdles and the tools to remove them.

In my experience, self-resistance comes after asking two questions, "What do I want?' and 'What do I do?"

Legitimate Question: "What do I want?"
Form of the Resistance: Things aren't so bad
Me1st Antidote: Give legitimacy to our own desires

This form of resistance is more common among leaders who are searching for the Next Big Challenge. It's the resistance after we ask the question, "What do I want?" because asking that question is both powerful and humbling, both exciting and fraught with fear.

One form of resistance here is the **temptation to convince ourselves that things aren't so bad**. In the PBS series *Downton Abbey*, one of the domestic servants is about to depart the household for another position. As she is speaking to the patriarch, Lord Crawley, she asks him, "Will you be happy?" In a classic example of self-generated resistance, he responds, "I have no right to be unhappy, which is almost the same…"

Bam! There it is…resistance.

The same thing happened to me once. My first job out of college was working as an assistant buyer for a department store in my hometown of Pittsburgh. Even though I knew it wasn't my life's work, it was an excellent first job. I learned so much about the business of business: the good, the bad, and the ugly. I worked for two outstanding bosses who mentored me, and I was making decent money. One day at lunch, my friend and fellow assistant buyer Brian said, "You know, this isn't so bad. It's somewhat interesting work and not too difficult. I could almost convince myself that it could be a career." I knew exactly what he meant. Relative comfort had appeared on the scene, and it was tempting for us to take full advantage of it.

The **Me1st Method** allows us great clarity and legitimacy to look at things as they really are. It allows us to recognize what we truly desire, by buying us the space and the freedom to be able to do that. When I do exercises in class that focus on thinking about dreams and desires, the most common feedback I hear is, "The most valuable thing about this exercise is that I had 20 minutes to actually ponder the question. I never get that in my day-to-day life."

Legitimate Question: "What do I want?"
Form of the Resistance: Frustration with the slow pace of change
Me1st Antidote: Grow in any circumstance

Second, there is the **temptation to become frustrated with the slow pace** of answering the "what do I want?" question. Look, if you wake up in the middle of the night tonight and your future is written out in full detail on your bedroom ceiling, great. I'm happy for you. For the rest of us, however, it doesn't work like that. Instead, it's a process marked by fits and starts, by dead-end roads and backtracking, by two steps forward and one step back.

When I was creating my first Personal Leadership Purpose Statement (see Chapters 6 and 11), I got stuck trying to identify and define my two core values—for several weeks! I just couldn't make up my mind. It got to the point where I would "try on" a certain value for a day and try to make my decisions according to it. I'd literally think, "OK, it's Tuesday. I am going to try on the value of security." It got to the point where I wanted to just throw the whole thing out! It was so damn frustrating! Remember in the introduction that I said this process involves hard work? Well, for me this is where some of the hardest work showed up. I am glad I persisted.

I see this form of resistance all the time with Next Big Challenge leaders—especially those that are in the process of taking on a bigger leadership role. Years ago, I was browsing a showroom at the High Point Furniture Market, the twice-yearly premier international furniture market in High Point, NC. I ran into Chris, my very first boss from my very first job at the department store. Although we still worked for the same company, we were now in different divisions and didn't see each other very much. Chris had recently been awarded a long-overdue promotion, but there he was on the showroom floor, examining a prototype sofa. Looking back, I now realize that Chris was doing what almost every leader does when faced with a new role and its accompanying challenges: going back and doing what he was really good at and what made him successful enough to earn that promotion. Chris did this for an afternoon, but he didn't lose sight of the big picture. Resistance showed up, but he was able to overcome it.

To overcome this resistance, taking the **Me1st Method** allows us to recognize that even when we're going at a slow pace, or even when we feel like we're moving backward, we're still learning. We're actually still moving forward. The **Me1st Method** allows us to win even when we lose because we're simply trying something. We're not beholden to the results, except that the results tell us something about ourselves.

Legitimate Question: "What do I do?"
Form of the Resistance: Knowing what to do, but not doing it
Me1st Antidote: Create momentum by doing it

The other forms of resistance from yourself have little to do with a lack of direction; instead, they have everything to do with fear about moving forward. These types of resistance are especially prevalent among leaders who are actively facing the Next Big Challenge and follow the question, "What do I do?"

The first form is **knowing what to do, but not doing it.** At some point in our journey, we obtain some clarity about what we're seeking to do. The picture might not be completely clear, but the leader at least knows what the next goal should be. Whether it's taking a new position, beginning a job search, reformulating the team, hiring new people, or beginning to develop the skills of having difficult conversations, we know what the next step should be.

Then resistance comes in the form of **not taking that step**. Resistance is too smart to say, "I won't ever take that step." No, in its usual underhanded way, resistance will instead say, "I won't take that step just yet. I'll do it *tomorrow*, but not *today*."

So, in other words, the biggest way to overcome resistance to doing things is just to do them.

Legitimate Question: "What do I do?"
Form of the Resistance: <u>Only</u> asking "what do I do?"
Me1st Antidote: Focus on being, not just doing

The other way that resistance shows up here is this: The leader **becomes so obsessed with asking the very legitimate question, "What do I do?" that they miss a different question that is probably more important; namely, "Who should I be?"** Leadership is striking a balance between doing and being because that sense of being ("Who I am?") forms the basis for what I do and, at the same time, what I do helps to shape who I am.

Resistance can come from being exclusively goal-oriented. I cringe every time I hear the words, "I have a bias for action" because I know what it often actually means, "I have a bias for staying as busy as possible so I can avoid the unpleasant work of looking at my own shit." Look, action is at the heart of leadership, but when action becomes a diversion from doing harder, more introspective work—that's resistance.

The **Me1st Method** overcomes this resistance by specifically looking at who we are as leaders, by looking at our own leader identity. Any decent leader development program includes a lot of information and a lot of doing, but **Me1st** has us slow down to think about *why*—and that *why* stems from who we are as leaders.

HURDLE #2: RESISTANCE FROM THE SYSTEM

No person is an island, and leadership does not happen in a vacuum. There's no such thing as context-free leadership because we are always dealing with real people in real situations. Moreover, leaders are always embedded in one or more social systems: 1:1 relationships with others, teams, organizations, families, communities, and society at large. Without exception, a Next Big Challenge leader both impacts and is impacted by their social systems. It's no surprise then that resistance can manifest itself within these systems. Let's look at two ways.

Legitimate Question: "What responsibilities do I have towards others?"
Form of the Resistance: Sit down! You're rocking the boat
Me1st Antidote: Focus on becoming emotionally mature within systems

Responsible leaders are constantly asking themselves, "What (legitimate) responsibilities do I have towards others who are in the same systems of which I am a part?" Whether it's a team, an organization, or a family, the wise leader will pay attention to those responsibilities and dutifully try to fulfill them.

That's good. That's right. That's ethical. That's responsible.

The resistance comes from the system and happens automatically, and we can sum it up with this phrase, **"Sit down! Don't rock the boat!"** Systems have a way of keeping people in line. Subtly and not-so-subtly, systems exert great pressure on people to play the same role over and over and over again. Systems have a knack for finding people, putting them into place, and then keeping them there. At the same time, people get comfortable playing a certain role and often unconsciously gravitate towards situations in which they can play that role, out of familiarity.

So if you're the fixer or the doer, and you suddenly say, "Hey, you know what? I'm going to let *you* take responsibility for that. I'm not going to do it"—well, watch out! The system is going to roar to keep you in line.

Or if you are the people pleaser—the person who seeks peace at all costs—and you decide to engage in some conflict or let some conflict happen, the system is going to push back against you and basically say, "No! We want you to step in and keep the peace because that's what you always do."

When the system is saying, "Sit down! Don't rock the boat!", a **Me1st** approach is vital because it allows us to see ourselves as autonomous, emotionally mature persons within that system. It allows us to make rational, thoughtful decisions about when we want to stand apart and when we want to connect. Our decision goes beyond a choice between being the lone ranger or being a mindless drone who acts according to what everyone else wants. Instead, the **Me1st Method** allows us to make more informed decisions and gives us the courage to follow through with what we decide regardless of the opinions of others.

Legitimate Question: "How do I pursue big goals?"
Form of the Resistance: The deck is stacked against your goals
Me1st Antidote: Focus on your inherent worth and agency to act

Every Next Big Challenge leader eventually asks, "What are my big goals?" and starts taking action. That's kind of the point of being a Next Big Challenge leader, right?

As soon as the leader starts taking action, they quickly realize that **all social systems have inherent mechanisms that inhibit some while enabling others.** In other words, there are structural elements of systems that can inhibit us as leaders. Often, these structural systems are related to demographic characteristics (with gender and race being the two most prevalent).

In situations in which we find the deck stacked against us, taking a **Me1st** approach amplifies our dignity, our worth, and our agency as individuals. It strengthens us with the courage to keep moving forward and to keep working to break down the structural elements. Perhaps most of all, it helps us to become more substantial, thoughtful people who are better able to link arms with others to pursue needed change.

HURDLE #3: RESISTANCE FROM OTHERS CLOSE TO YOU

Perhaps the form of resistance that is easiest to sense or feel is resistance from others who are close to you. While it may be easier to *sense*, it is not always easier to *identify*. It can be difficult to clarify what we should and should not be expecting from others, and what they should and should not be expecting from us. Let's take a look at two specific questions and their accompanying forms of resistance.

Legitimate Question: "What support should I seek from others?"
Form of the Resistance: Near enemies of healthy support
Me1st Antidote: Ask for what you need. Better yet, supply it yourself.

One very legitimate question that Next Big Challenge leaders ought to be asking is, "What type of support can I get from others who are close to me?" We absolutely want to seek out support from others. Leading is hard work. Working through a challenge as a leader is even harder. We need support, and there is no good reason to walk this road alone (by the way, this is why we have peer-to-peer support and coaching support built right into the **Me1st Academy**).

Healthy support is vital, but here's the form of resistance with this topic. It's what author Brené Brown, drawing on Buddhist concepts, refers to as a 'near enemy'[2]. **A near enemy is a form of support that** looks and feels much like the healthy support we desire but is actually not the real thing. In fact, it ends up causing more harm. Let me give you two examples.

First, resistance comes from **desiring empathy from others but instead receiving only sympathy.** *Empathy* is a legitimate, healthy form of support that involves recognizing another's emotional state and reflecting it back from a place of shared humanity. It does not mean that we get sucked into others' problems and end up feeling their emotions for them. Instead, it means that we come alongside to create and maintain a healthy human connection.

As a near enemy, *sympathy* is a sort of pseudo-empathy. It's saying words that we think are helpful, but it's from a distance. Let's say that you've just had a rough meeting with your boss and you're visibly upset. You see a co-worker, and instead of saying an empathetic, "Oh yeah, that sucks. I have been there and it is not fun," your co-worker responds with a sympathetic, "Awww...bless your heart" (which my Southern friends tell me is actually code for "mmm...that's rough, but I really don't relate, or care").

The other big form of this resistance is **receiving advice instead of actual support.** When we mention a challenge, people are only too happy to jump in and start offering advice. When it is desired and informed, advice can be helpful, of course. However, when it is just spouted out as an automatic response, it is a near enemy.

This happened to me just this morning. One of my kids is not feeling well today and my wife happened to text a family member to relay that information. The response from that family member was "Oh, well, better start pumping the vitamin C and the zinc." All right, maybe that's decent medical advice, but it wasn't needed. It wasn't wanted. In fact, it had more to do with the person's need to be "helpful" than providing actual support. Actual support might have been some empathy or, better yet, an offer to provide desired help.

A **Me1st** approach allows us to recognize the specific types of support that we need. It helps us to speak up and to advocate for ourselves to receive that support. It also helps us by enabling us to set boundaries and say, "That is not helpful." Better yet, a **Me1st** approach trains us to equip ourselves to be our own first option when we have needs.

Legitimate Question: "How do I inspire others to action?"
Form of the Resistance: People do not buy what we are selling
Me1st Antidote: Your primary job is to display emotional maturity

> "Leadership is the art of getting someone else to do something you want done because he wants to do it."
> —DWIGHT D. EISENHOWER

Leadership always involves motivating others or in some way inspiring others to take some form of action. Again, that is a legitimate concern. Leaders need to be asking themselves, "How do I inspire my team? How do I motivate other people?"

Resistance, though, comes in **believing that if we can just figure out the right levers to pull and the right buttons to push that things will magically fall into place.** People will automatically respond to our attempts to influence them. When that doesn't happen, we feel like we're not making progress. Even worse, it might undermine our very confidence as leaders.

Following the Me1st Method helps us to recognize that, while motivation may be important, it is not the primary function of a leader. Instead, my first job as a leader is to bring an emotionally mature presence to the system.

Emotional maturity means being able to think and act independently while remaining connected to others. It's a different point of view for sure, and we'll talk more about that in a later chapter.

SOME CONCLUDING THOUGHTS

Back in the introduction to this book, I wrote that the message of this book could be summed up in three points. Let's take a moment to revisit them in light of what we have just discussed.

1. Facing the Next Big Challenge requires hard work for leaders

In this chapter, we zeroed in on these special challenges and gave them a name: *resistance.* The challenges and hurdles are common, and we should expect them. Moreover, we should see them as signs that we are on the right track. It's sort of like beginning a new weight lifting program. You know you are going to be sore after the first few sessions, but you don't see that soreness as a sign to stop. You're encouraged, because you know that soreness means your efforts have made an impact.

2. This work is best accomplished by following the **Me1st Method**

Besides giving you a map of the neighborhood of resistance, I also introduced the concept that focusing on yourself first is the single best way to overcome the various forms of resistance. In subsequent chapters, we will break down the entire **Me1st Method**, but for now— if I've done my job—you are at least open to the notion that it is a viable way forward.

3. This work is easier and faster with support and guidance

We will get into the nitty-gritty of finding and using support later on in Chapter 10. But in this chapter, we began to build the foundation by examining what resistance looks like when we seek support from others who are close to us.

Before we get into how the **Me1st Method** actually works, we need to take a look at the single biggest question that Next Big Challenge leaders ask, the "quick fix" answers to this question, and why they don't work.

4

THE SEDUCTIVE TRAP OF THE QUICK-FIX

"Short cuts make long delays."
— J.R.R. Tolkien

PROBLEMS LEADERS FACE

I have the privilege of working with a lot of motivated and capable people, both as a coach and as a professor. I have many conversations with many different people—everything from students hanging around after class to ask a burning question to initial discussions with potential **Me1st Academy** clients. Through these conversations, I have come to recognize what I believe to be the single biggest stumbling block to Next Big Challenge leaders. I think it even has a name:

"How Do I Fix My Problem, Right Now?"

People seek help when there is a problem to solve. Among leaders in the workplace, that problem usually presents itself in one of a few predictable ways:

1. Employee retention

While retaining talent is an ongoing challenge for all companies, as I write these words (in early 2022) the job market is especially challenging for employers. Leaders have multiple open positions and/or are in imminent danger of having other team members leave. They also see the spiraling effects starting to kick in: exhaustion and burnout among remaining team members, increased pressure to deliver results, and impacts of short-staffing at other firms (think about shipping delays, etc.).

2. Performance

Fixing the problem of underperforming employees is another common challenge. By the time they get to me, leaders have tried all sorts of things. Pep talks. Incentives. Performance improvement plans. Listening. Cajoling. You name it, they've tried it.

3. Demonstrating my own value

For many leaders, things are generally going well, but they want more. They are ready for the next promotion or assignment, but—for whatever reason—they are being passed over. Sometimes, their own bosses are encouraging them to seek out coaching or other forms of help. Other times, it is the leaders themselves who are doing so. Phrases like "developing executive presence" or "being taken seriously" get bandied about.

Listen, I get it. I respect the problems, and I respect the need to have them solved ASAP. People don't work with me—not as a professor, not as a coach—unless they have problems to solve or mountains to climb. And I wish—oh, how I wish!—that I had a magic cure for them.

But I don't.

And I don't think anyone really does, but that doesn't stop leaders from trying for a quick fix (which is very understandable) or leadership consultants trying to sell people on a shortcut (which is simply not honest).

ATTEMPTED QUICK FIXES

1. Focus on developing new skills or obtaining new knowledge

Pick up the latest issue of the *Wall Street Journal* or *Fast Company* or go to your favorite leadership guru's blog and I bet you will see a version of "Leadership Skills for the 21st Century" or something similar. Similarly, the multibillion-dollar leader development industry is obsessed with skill development and knowledge acquisition.

There's a good reason for this focus: skills represent the most tangible, most visible forms of doing leadership. For example, I can attend a one-day training on developing active listening skills. If the training is done well, it will include lots of good information. It will include opportunities to practice. It will even include pre-training and post-training assessments in order to show that participants have improved —thus showing the value of the training.

Similarly, obtaining new knowledge is easy to understand, and knowledge is easy to obtain. Books, podcasts, speeches, and training classes all provide an easy avenue to knowledge acquisition.

In short, obtaining new skills and knowledge is often viewed as the ultimate "fast-forward card" to improved leader effectiveness. The underlying (and often unspoken) mantra is, "If I display (New Skill) or learn (New Knowledge), then people will respond the way I desire."

2. Focus on motivating others

Almost as prevalent as skill development and knowledge acquisition is a focus on motivating other people. In fact, in many leadership models, motivation is a skill set in and of itself. Pick up a biography (or, better yet, an autobiography) of a famous business or military leader. I bet you will see pages and pages about how they motivated other people. You will see phrases like, "I didn't manage people. I motivated them."

Again, there is a good reason for this focus. In general, motivated people tend to perform better. One of the most-studied and best-supported models of motivation, goal-setting theory, demonstrates that having specific yet achievable goals along with some sort of feedback mechanism leads to higher performance.[1]

The underlying (and often unspoken) mantra is, "If I can just motivate others better, they will respond the way I desire."

3. Change the situation by switching roles or switching people

A somewhat different tactic is to hit the reset button every time there is a significant challenge to one's leadership. This tactic can work. Think about sports coaches who take a new job every 1 or 2 years to work their way up the ladder. They achieve a certain level of success and then hit the road before their performance regresses to the mean.

An alternative version is a leader whose team changes on a continual basis. People come in, they perform, they hit a rough patch, and they are let go or quit.

The underlying (and often unspoken) mantra is, "If people aren't responding the way I desire, then I will just find a new set of people."

THE SEDUCTION

We need to recognize two things about these attempted quick fixes—two things that are very seductive:

1. **They do have a role to play**

None of these things is bad. Quite the opposite:

- Leaders absolutely must be concerned with honing their current skills and developing new ones
- Obtaining knowledge is vital (after all, you are reading this book to obtain knowledge)
- By default, leaders have a major impact on the motivation of those they lead
- By definition, being a Next Big Challenge leader means making changes, and sometimes those changes mean moving to a new role/ new company/ new career or making personnel changes to one's team

So it's not that these tactics are bad. In fact, I bet you have tried all of them and probably had some level of success in doing so. The problem is not with the tactic per se; instead, the problem *is* **using one or more of these tactics as the <u>first option</u> undermines the deep introspective work that is needed to create clear, lasting results.**

2. **Each of them does have an element of <u>self-focused</u> action**

Maybe you were convinced of the need to take a Meıst approach before you ever picked up this book, or maybe you've warmed to the idea from what you have read so far. In fact, you might be thinking, "I am almost always focusing on myself":

- I read books. I listen to podcasts. I go to training

- I am constantly seeking ways to improve myself
- I am always looking for new opportunities

Good for you! I sincerely mean that. These are important and honorable things. But therein lies the seduction. Each of these actions promises a quick fix if you just:

- Do more
- Do something different
- Do something faster or better

And I don't doubt this: you're pretty damn good at getting things done. Most leaders are. Yet, you now find yourself facing the Next Big Challenge and are realizing that these actions are not enough. Let me try to put words to this feeling you might be having:

"I can't simply *do* my way through this challenge"

Does that resonate with you?

In other words, you can't just perform your way to a successful outcome. You can't just find the right skill training. You can't just hit the right motivational button in others. And you can't just reshuffle the board to assure success.

If you still believe that you can simply perform your way to success, then I sincerely wish you well—but I am not the right person to help you. The rest of this book? Probably not much help to you. The Me1st Academy? Not a good fit right now.

If you are still open to the possibility that a true self-focused approach can help, then I present…

CONCLUDING THOUGHTS: THE ME1ST METHOD
ALTERNATIVE

If the **Me1st Method** isn't just about me as the leader taking action, then what is it actually about?

It's a process. It's a philosophy. And it's a method that is backed up by a good deal of research. So let's take a sneak peek at what is coming in Part 2:

- **Motivate**—Discovering what you are trying to accomplish: the clear results for yourself, your team, and your organization. If you are trying to **find** your Next Big Challenge, this step is vital. If you are trying to figure out if the challenge you already have aligns with who you are and desire to become, it is also for you.
- **Educate & Evaluate**—Learning about effective leadership (including knowledge and skills) and how to accurately assess where you are as a leader right now. This step is vital for preparing to **face** the Next Big Challenge.
- **1** thing at a time—reminder that **facing** the Next Big Challenge takes time and effort, so keep it manageable
- **Strategize**—Creating a plan to close the gap between where you are and where you wish to be. Developing your own best thinking in this way is a powerful step in **facing** the Next Big Challenge.
- **Test**—Experimenting, acting in its proper time, and adopting a "no failure" mentality until you **embrace** the Next Big Challenge

We also discuss a critical ingredient that, while not a quick fix or a fast forward, can make the process faster, easier, and more efficient: finding proper support.

I'm really excited to lay out everything for you to consider, so on to Part 2!

Part II:

The **Me1st** Method

5

THE SCIENCE OF LEADER DEVELOPMENT

"There's nothing so practical as a good theory." —KURT LEWIN

B efore we discuss the **Me1st Method** beginning in the next chapter, I want to show you *why* this approach works. I want to pull back the curtain, Wizard of Oz style. It's actually a combination of several different bodies of research. You know by now that I'm a professor, so you know that I teach and do research. In contrast to physicists and chemists (who get all the easy problems), I study people (and people are really strange sometimes). Put simply, I'm a social scientist.

I do research about leadership, so everything that I do in my coaching practice and with my training is related to scientifically validated, peer-reviewed research. That doesn't mean it's the ultimate end-all, be-all truth, never to change. No, of course not. That's not how science works.

What it does mean is that there is a lot of credible evidence behind the things that we do and the approach that we take. In this particular program, the **Me1st Method**, there are four different theories that we're going to rely upon.

Now, please let me take a moment and give you the same disclaimer that I give my students about theory. Sometimes when we hear the word theory, we think, "Oh, that's not something that actually works. It's just a bunch of ideas."

That's incorrect. Why? Because theory—good theory—is an explanatory mechanism. It explains not only what's happening, but *why* it happens. And when we understand why something happens, then we can predict what's going to happen. Sometimes we can even impact it.

So, when I say theory, I'm actually talking about something that's quite practical, not just pie-in-the-sky, ivory tower kind of stuff. When we know theory, we can use theory. Cool? OK.

BOWEN FAMILY SYSTEMS THEORY

Leadership does not happen in a vacuum; after all, leadership is about leading *other people*. At its heart, leadership involves a relationship between at least two people. And anytime we have at least two people, we also have a social system. Therefore, we need to understand how social systems function in order to really understand how leadership functions. Whether we are talking about just two people, or a team of many people, or an entire organization, or a family, or a community group, some basic rules apply to all of them. In this regard, **Bowen Family Systems Theory** acts as our guide. This theory originated with Dr. Murray Bowen's work with families, but I find it helpful because it offers great insight into how *all* social systems function, including organizations and businesses.[1]

No matter the type of system, the key variable that we want to focus on is *anxiety*, defined as the automatic response to a threat in the environment, whether that threat is real and imminent (acute anxiety) or is very unlikely or perhaps even imagined (chronic anxiety). Again, regardless of the type, anxiety is the automatic, reflexive response to a threat.

Before we go much further, it's worth pointing something out: periods of challenge are full of anxiety, both for the person(s) actually facing the challenge and for the systems that are being impacted. Next Big Challenge leaders are particularly at risk for anxiety to derail their plans and dreams.

Let's take just one type of challenge—starting a new role—as an example. Perhaps you've just been promoted from a team leader to leading an entire department. You have your own anxieties to deal with ("Am I right for this role? Can I be effective in this role?"), and the system creates its own anxieties. Some members of the system may look to you to be the heroic savior who will make everything right, while others see you as an incompetent newbie who is going to strip them of power.

To put it bluntly, a Next Big Challenge leader is usually seconds away from someone's anxiety shit storm—their own, or someone else in the system.

So, with that happy thought in mind, let's take a look at the ways anxiety shows up in systems.

Five Automatic Responses to Anxiety

Now, here's what is both disheartening and hopeful at the same time: systems will react to anxiety in one of just a few dysfunctional—but predictable—ways. If we can understand what these automatic anxiety actions are and figure out some strategies for dealing with them, then we have put ourselves in a much, much better position to be able to resolve them effectively. Let's take a look at them one at a time.

Conflict

Anxiety often results in conflict, which is simply a state of disagreement based on real or perceived differences in needs, beliefs, ideas, or resources. There are three different types of conflict that we can run into: *Task conflict* is conflict over the goals that we are pursuing, *process conflict* is conflict over how we will go about doing those tasks, and *relationship conflict* is conflict directly with another person(s). The research about conflict shows us that sometimes it can be helpful and can actually produce some good outcomes, but only if that conflict is task or process conflict in low to moderate levels, for a short period of time. However, if conflict is too high, lasts too long, or is any type of relational conflict, it's always unhealthy. It's not helpful.

Distancing

Anxiety can also be handled through distancing, in which one party avoids the other party, or both parties avoid each other. We see distancing acted out by ignoring communications, making sure that the two parties are rarely if ever in physical proximity, or going out of the way to avoid talking about whatever challenges and problems exist. In extreme cases, distancing can result in *cutoff*, in which the relationship between two parties is severed (think of two estranged family members).

Closeness

The third anxiety relief mechanism is the opposite of distancing: closeness. More accurately, it's extreme closeness to the point of being fused with one another. It's two parties coming together and being so closely aligned with one another that you don't know where one party ends and the other one begins. It's almost essentially as if two people are functioning as the same person.

The result is neither person is truly doing their own independent thinking, but the closeness that the two parties feel brings great relief from the anxiety in the system.

Third-Party Focus

The fourth way systems respond to anxiety is through a focus on a third party. For example, think about a husband and wife who are having marital issues. Instead of working on those issues, they relieve their anxiety by focusing intently on a particular child. The child's activities, achievements, issues, ailments, and illnesses are all fair game for inordinate focus from the parents, as a way of avoiding their own issues. We see this all the time in the workplace as well. If there's anxiety between two parties, they will pick out a third party to focus on—perhaps as a scapegoat or as a distraction. That third party need not be a person; it could also be a big project that needs to be done or a threat from a competitor.

Over- and Under-Functioning

The fifth possible response is what we call over-functioning and under-functioning. This occurs when one party starts to take on responsibilities and tasks the other party should be doing. For example, in response to anxiety or crisis, the boss jumps in and starts doing the job of one or more of the team members (over-functioning). And at the same time, the team member is like, "That's pretty cool. I'm going to go ahead and let the boss do that" (under-functioning). You then end up with a situation where one party is doing things that the other party really should be doing. The over-functioner ends up burned out, and the under-functioner ends up impoverished.

Special Note: In my experience, the most common role that otherwise effective leaders default to is that of the over-functioner, because most leaders tend to be high achievers. They get stuff done. They have expertise. They get results. And they are willing to do whatever it takes to achieve—including jumping in to save the day because it is easier and more efficient in the short term.

If you'd like to see these five automatic responses in action, take a second and re-read the examples of Nancy, Sam, Angela, and Mike in Chapter 1. How many automatic responses can you spot? (Heck, I'll give you a freebie: over-functioning is present in all of them).

Things Get Complex

Notice that each of these five anxiety responses involves two parties (often two people). But the overall situation is more complex than just dealing with two parties. This little fact—which I unpack below—

makes things more challenging for leaders, but it also reveals the key for creating our forward momentum and clear results.

In a nutshell, the two parties are not what we should be focusing on when we're trying to understand systems.

Instead, we want to be looking for three-party systems—or, more simply, triangles. Three-party triangles are the most fundamental *stable* building block in social systems. It's sort of like having a stable stool or a tripod—you need three legs to keep it steady.

Here's an example: think of the last time you noticed conflict between two people (and you might have been one of the two, or simply an outside observer). What happened? My guess is that one or both people automatically sought to pull in a third party in order to relieve that anxiety between them. They tried to get their boss to take sides, or each of them tried to find another colleague to commiserate with. Or maybe they even realized that the conflict was not helpful, and they sought out some sort of "common enemy" to focus on, which had the effect of burying the conflict and replacing it with a hot-wired closeness around this common "threat".

Systems function in triangles, but the news actually gets even more complex than that. It's not just one triangle we have to consider, because social systems are made up of a network of interlocking triangles. Through these interlocking triangles, anxiety gets passed around like a hot potato.

Let's consider an example. Let's say you work in a small company that is owned equally by two brothers who happen to be in conflict with one another. In order to alleviate that conflict, they pull in a third party: your boss. They focus on your boss as the source of their conflict, even though it's not your boss's fault and your boss really didn't have anything to do with it. As the old saying goes, "Shit rolls downhill."

As a result, the anxiety that should be managed between the two brothers gets pushed down to your boss in this "owner-owner-your boss" triangle. Now your boss is taking that same anxiety and focusing it on you, by being short-tempered, unreasonable, and micro-managing. In order to alleviate this pressure, you are now trying to pull in your coworker who's on the same team. You build an alliance with your coworker centered on what a jerk your boss is being. The formation of this "boss-you-coworker" triangle brings some relief to you, but also passes along the anxiety to your co-worker (who perhaps now goes home and kicks the dog—yet another triangle).

See what happened? The anxiety that actually belongs to the two owners gets pushed to your boss so that the owners find some relief. Your boss then pushes it to you, in order to get some relief. You in turn pull in your co-worker, to get some relief. This network of interlocking triangles allows problems at the top to filter down through the entire system. Over time, this dynamic takes on a life of its own, to the point where no one can even remember where the anxiety actually originated.

Remember: these are automatic responses. No one in this scenario is Dr. Evil planning to set off an anxiety bomb throughout the company. We need not judge the individuals in terms of intent or action; instead, we are focusing on the *system itself*.

But Good News: There is a Key to Unlocking Triangles

The good news is this: once we learn to recognize triangles, we unlock the power to use them to our advantage. (And by the way, once you start to look for triangles, you will see them everywhere—and you can't un-see them, either).

In order to stop this dynamic of anxiety being passed around in social systems, there needs to be at least one person who is willing to develop and display some emotional maturity (to use Bowen language, to be a better-differentiated self). There needs to be just one person who is willing to explore options and put forth their own best thinking. One person to make a stand if necessary, and to act alone if necessary, but at the same time remain connected to the other people in the system. One person who is willing to work through conflict without becoming either distant or overly close. One person who refuses to over- or under-function or give in to the quick fix of roping in a third party. When even one differentiated, thoughtful, emotionally mature individual shows up, the anxiety will begin to resolve itself, because it's put back on the parties that actually should own it. They're forced to do something with it because there's nowhere for it to go.

The really good news is that person **can** be you. In fact, as a leader, it **needs** to be you. What's more, as a Next Big Challenge leader, it **must** be you.

Going back to our example, it would have been best if one of the two owners put a stop to the anxiety spread by displaying emotional maturity. The next best option would have been for your boss to refuse to take it on. The third best option would have been for you to stop the spread. Even though it would have been quicker and more efficient for the change to happen at the top, **you still have the power to impact the system through your own actions,** no matter what position you hold in the organization.

This is exactly the reason why we take the self-focused Me1st approach to leader development in this book. This is exactly why my leader development community is called the Me1st Academy.

I'll be even blunter here (but I am saying it in the kindest possible way): **if you are not willing to do the hard work of developing yourself first, you have no business leading other people. You also can't reasonably expect the challenge you are facing to end successfully.**

No matter what your goals or desired outcomes are, remember this: **you yourself are your single greatest leverage point in any social system.** Want to change the system? Focus on yourself first.

But how? Well, I am glad you asked. Let's turn to our other two theories to explain what we should do, and why.

INTENTIONAL CHANGE THEORY

With our new knowledge of systems in mind, the next theory we call upon is **Intentional Change Theory**, or ICT.[2] ICT is an approach to how individuals grow and change, making the case that there are five different discoveries that a person needs to go through in order to change.

- The first discovery is their **ideal self**; in other words, what is it that I would like to become if I could be all that I desire to be? It is discovering what that "ideal me" looks like in an ideal world.
- The second discovery is their **actual self**; in other words, what am I today? How am I functioning today? How am I acting today? This is where getting some feedback from others can be helpful.

70

- The third discovery is understanding what the gap is between the ideal self and the actual self, and then creating a strategy to close that gap, moving from where we are today (actual self) to where we'd like to be tomorrow (ideal self).
- The fourth discovery is to simply experiment—to take some ideas from that strategy and put them into practice and see what happens.
- And then the fifth discovery is discovering support along the way. This is where coaching and peer support come into play.

MULTIPLE INTELLIGENCES RESEARCH

In the 1980's psychologists Robert Sternberg and Douglas Detterman proposed a unique idea to the field of psychology; namely, that intelligence consists of more than just cognitive (that is, thinking-based) ability[3]. Over time, the research behind this notion has grown significantly. The notion that intelligence actually consists of several components forms the basis for several fairly recognizable theories of intelligence, including social intelligence, cultural intelligence, and—perhaps the one that is most recognizable to leaders—emotional intelligence.

The current consensus among these different bodies of research is that intelligence actually consists of four primary parts:

- **Motivational Intelligence**—Recognizes that intelligence is *motivationally driven*; people have a specific purpose in mind that fuels their desire and effort to become more intelligent.
- **Cognitive Intelligence**—What we typically think of first with respect to intelligence, this aspect refers to the **knowledge** and knowledge structures that individuals possess.

- **Metacognitive Intelligence**—Involves the processes individuals use to acquire, understand, and apply knowledge. Put another way, it's "thinking about thinking" and is often closely associated with *strategy*.
- **Behavioral Intelligence**—Focuses on an individual's action-oriented capabilities; in other words, it involves what a person *can actually do*.

These two combined theories explain why we've structured the program the way that we have—the **Me1st Method** is based directly on this research. Both point to having the same four components (plus the additional component of support, as articulated in Intentional Change Theory). As we journey through the next four chapters, you will see glimpses of both of these theories throughout.

SELF-DETERMINATION THEORY

Now we understand systems, as well as a scientific process to follow, but what actually needs to change within us in order to create the forward momentum that creates clear results and lasting change? The theory that we draw upon to answer this question is called **self-determination theory**.[4] Basically, self-determination theory says that an individual's motivation, including the motivation to continue to grow, is driven by three innate needs—needs that we are all born with by virtue of the fact of being human.

According to self-determination theory, the first need is *autonomy*, which is acting with a sense of volition and choice as well as having some actual influence over what's happening around us and to us. The second need is *relatedness*; the sense of feeling cared for by others and also having the opportunity to care for others. Relatedness is all about that human connection and caring for one another. The third innate need is *competence;* that is, feeling effective in both our words and our actions. We need to feel like we can actually do something and do it fairly well—that we have some level of mastery.

So those are our three needs (autonomy, relatedness, and competence), but here's the key to these needs actually motivating us:

In order for these three needs to motivate us, we want to satisfy them *intrinsically.* In other words, we need to get to a place where we derive our own value and satisfaction from pursuing and meeting our needs for autonomy, relatedness, and competence. We are pursuing them for *their own sake,* and not for any sort of external reward.

Again, I don't want you to miss this point: **the key here is that in order to satisfy these three needs, it needs to be done in a way that it's self-directed and self-determined. As individuals, we need to satisfy these needs for ourselves.** It's not something that can be just handed to us—it's not like somebody can just, you know, turn over the keys to the car and say, "Here you go, you're autonomous and competent now! Go relate to people!"

Don't get me wrong: other people can help. But the role of others in this process is to provide support rather than do the work for you. They can help set the context for you to meet these needs and it's up to you to actually meet them. That's what creates clear results.

All right—so that's the explanation about what actually develops. But I want to take self-determination theory just one step further. Instead of using the terms that are from the scientific research (autonomy, relatedness, and competence), I would expand each one of those a bit, for two reasons. One, I think those terms are a little bit academic jargon-ish, and I think that there are some better words that we use every day that are probably better descriptors. Second, I also think that those terms are a little bit too narrow. I think it does us well to expand each one of them somewhat and to take a more expansive view.

So instead of autonomy, I like the term **freedom**. Freedom includes autonomy, certainly, but it also includes a sense of exploration and play and seeking joy in our circumstances. It includes setting appropriate boundaries and defining, "Here's who I am and what I will do, and here's who I am not and what I will not do."

Instead of relatedness, I like to refer to **connectedness.** It certainly includes that sense of caring for others and being cared for, but it's also a bigger mindset of creating and supporting the structures that make it possible for everyone to both care for others and to be cared for more systematically.

Finally, instead of just competence, I want to think in terms of **wisdom**. Wisdom includes competence in the form of practical wisdom, but it also includes the knowledge behind that competence— the facts that we know, skills that we have and can employ, and also the way we go about feeling about things. Wisdom also includes having a high level of emotional maturity. Think of the wisest people that you know: they know a lot of things, they can do a lot of things, but there's also this almost palpable sense of peace about them. They have the maturity to be able to regulate those emotions.

As we journey through the **Me1st Method**, you will notice that everything we do leads to one or more of these outcomes.

CONCLUDING THOUGHTS

We can sum up this chapter with just a few key points:

1. Leadership—like all forms of human relationship—takes place within social systems. Therefore, understanding how social systems

function—especially our own role within them—allows us to see why the **Me1st Method** is important.

2. The **Me1st Method** itself—which we look at in the next four chapters—is based on two overlapping research-based theories: Intentional Change Theory and Multiple Intelligences. As such, it is supported by a good deal of evidence that we need to understand what motivates us, have a firm grasp on where we are and what we need, develop a strategy, and test out ideas with action.

3. Individuals are motivated to fulfill intrinsic needs for freedom, wisdom, and connectedness. The **Me1st Method** is designed to increase freedom, wisdom, and connectedness, both for individual leaders and their teams/organizations.

OK…I'm feeling like it's time to unpack the **Me1st Method** properly —so let's do that now.

6

FINDING THE NEXT BIG CHALLENGE: MOTIVATE

THE ME1ST METHOD, STEP 1

"If you don't know where you're going, any road will get you there"
−SOMETHING LEWIS CARROLL PROBABLY NEVER SAID

W here are we going? And how are we getting there?

This line is an oft-used paraphrase of the exchange between Alice and the Cheshire Cat in *Alice in Wonderland*. I have even used it myself in my leadership classes. We are all, as Alice desires, looking to get somewhere. The question is: where? And, once we have a sense of where, we are all trying to figure out the next question: how? Knowing where we are going—or at least knowing where we desire to go— provides the overall orientation for our journey. Caring about where we are going provides the fuel to get there.

OK. Great. But so what?

The 'so what' has to do with motivation, which is all about the effort put forth to accomplish something. Motivation consists of three parts: *direction* (what the effort is directed towards), *intensity* (how much effort is put forth), and *persistence* (how long the effort is put forth). Knowing where we are going provides the direction of our effort while caring about where we are going provides the intensity and persistence of our effort. When we both know and care, we provide ourselves with all of the necessary ingredients to sustain our motivation.

Simple enough, right?

But what does it look like in practice? How do you take this nice little idea and make it into something useful? **How do you find your Next Big Challenge, or how do you make sense of the Next Big Challenge that has already found you?** The Next Big Challenge is not an end itself, but is rather a milestone for a longer journey, a chapter in a bigger story.

In this chapter, we consider answering this question at three different levels: the personal (individual) level, the team level, and the organizational level. Note that as we do so, we are developing motivational intelligence and working through the first discovery from Intentional Change Theory. But we are also expanding this idea to include discovering the ideal team and the ideal organization.

PERSONAL LEVEL: DISCOVERING YOUR PURPOSE AS A LEADER

The best way that I know to discover our ideal self and to provide the motivation for the work we must do is by constructing a Personal Leadership Purpose Statement (PLPS)—a concise and living two-page document that serves as our leadership constitution. A PLPS serves several purposes:

- First and foremost, it provides tremendous guidance towards finding and making sense of our Next Big Challenge

- During the most challenging times (a.k.a. our anxiety shit storms), it reminds us of our ultimate aspirations
- When opportunities arise, it guides us to make good decisions
- When actual danger appears, it protects us by giving us tools to overcome the danger

In Chapter 11, I will walk you through how to construct a PLPS. For now, though, I will simply outline its three main parts.

The Three Parts of a Personal Leadership Purpose Statement

1. Vision of Ideal Life

The first part is a vivid portrayal of our ideal life at some point in the future (I suggest 5 years, but feel free to define your own meaningful timeline). It should include both professional and personal aspects.

Here's one line from my own PLPS (focused on the professional): "I lead a team of pracademics…" Pracademics are people who deliberately focus both on research and practice (either professors who practice, or practitioners [coaches and consultants] who draw from research). These are my people because they have a foot in research and practice—and, as a result, are best equipped to do each of them.

Here's another line from my PLPS (personal this time): "We enjoy daily conversations around the kitchen counter." As in many homes, the kitchen is the hub of activity in my house. Several years ago, we did a renovation to open up the kitchen and make a counter space big enough to seat all 6 of us. Now, it is where we do most of our eating and important communication. I imagine that continuing and increasing in the years to come. For me, it represents the good life in a very compelling way.

· · ·

2. Mission in Life

If our vision of the ideal life is a painting, then our mission in life is the frame. It helps to focus attention on the painting itself (the vision), but it also serves as a boundary between the painting and the rest of the world. We can't do it all, so what are the boundaries around what we can and will do? What will we focus on? What will we avoid? In short, how will we work to achieve our ideal life?

A clearly defined mission helps us to do several things, all of which have a direct bearing on finding the Next Big Challenge. First, it gives us direction to say *yes* to the very best opportunities. Second, it helps us to **resist the temptation** to say yes to potentially bad or harmful choices. Third, and perhaps most importantly, it gives us permission to say *no* to what might be very good opportunities, but ones that are not suited to us.

Let me give you an example from my own mission statement in my PLPS: "I am responsible to God, to myself, to my circle of intimates, to my clients and associates, and to those who are placed in my life—in that order." I put this line in to remind myself that not everyone gets my time and attention in equal parts. There is a pecking order, and this is it.

Remember, a well-defined mission in life helps to tell us what to do when we are faced with opportunities.

3. Two Foundational Values

We now have the painting itself (vision) and a frame around it (mission), but what makes the portrait unique? At least one element is the choice of paint itself, the colors. Values serve the same function in our PLPS by further defining and refining our intended actions. Values are simply ways of doing (e.g., efficiency or authenticity) or states of being (e.g., security or peace) that we hold as especially important. Values serve as a day-in, day-out guide for helping us to live according to our mission in support of our vision. Here is a key point: **if you cannot relate a possible Next Big Challenge to at least one of your values, it is not a challenge you ought to be pursuing.**

Here's the trick to this part: define two—and only two—primary values. The fewer values you focus on, the more useful they are. We will unpack why this is so in Chapter 11. [1]

My two values are Freedom (which I define as throwing off unhealthy restraints and embracing exploration, experimenting, and play) and Wisdom (which I define as the pursuit of being excellent at knowing, being, feeling, and doing).

That's it. Three simple parts that together can have a profound impact. Notice how it helps us to focus on creating wisdom (by thinking about the future in advance), freedom (by helping to define what we will and will not do), and connectedness (by including our aspirations of how we will relate to family, friends, and professional colleagues). I read my PLPS almost every day, and it acts as my own personal constitution —the foundational document that describes who I aspire to be and what I aspire to do when I interact with the world and people around me. One might even say that it is the First Document of the **Me1st Method.**

TEAM LEVEL: CREATING CONDITIONS FOR HIGH PERFORMANCE

Your Next Big Challenge might be related to your team. Perhaps it is molding a bunch of individuals into a team (as Coach Herb Brooks did with the 1980 U.S. Men's Olympic Hockey Team as depicted in the movie *Miracle*) or getting a team to shift focus suddenly and decisively (like Commander Melissa Lewis in the movie *The Martian*). Whatever the challenge, it is likely to focus on or at least impact your team. So let's learn more.

First of all, what is a team? Let's define our terms. My definition of a team is **a collection of interdependent individuals who are working together for some sort of a common purpose.** One of the questions that I often hear in my classes is, "Hey, is there a difference between a team and a group?" I'll often use those terms quite interchangeably, but I think that the distinction is simply the level of interdependence among the different people on the team. Very interdependent individuals tend towards being a team, and less interdependent individuals tend towards being a group.

With that in mind, I'm going to assume that you are leading a team in some way. This might be a more traditional view of a team in the sense that you have people reporting directly to you and you are responsible for leading them, but it can also be a little bit more informal.

A more informal team would be something more like a project manager, where you're leading for a particular project and you've got people on that project team. They don't directly report to you in an organizational sense, but you need them to all contribute in order to bring the project to fruition.

I also want to cast a bit of a broader net here for defining teams. Let's say that you are a solo entrepreneur or you're leading a group of volunteers; in other words, something that doesn't quite fit that traditional model. Many of the things that we're going to be talking about apply to you, but you just have to think a little bit more expansively. Even if you are a one-person shop with your business, I would argue that you're still leading in some way. Perhaps you're using a virtual assistant, or you've outsourced your marketing or some part of the business—you're still doing team-like things with those people. When you collaborate with clients, you have created a temporary team (maybe even just with two people).

Two Characteristics of All High-Performing Teams

There is no shortage of information about how effective teams function.

Books. Articles. Podcasts. Other books.

Knowledge about how teams function is incredibly important; in fact, we create and share this type of knowledge in the Me1st Academy. I don't mean to downplay or ignore this knowledge; however, for the purposes of motivation and understanding how to discover what an ideal, high-functioning team looks like, we need to start in a different place.

With that in mind, let's start with what I think are sort of the "lowest common denominator" team characteristics. These are the two overarching issues that all teams need to account for (and by the way, if there are team problems, this is where they will show up). In Chapter 12, we will explore these principles further in the process of creating a team charter, but for now, we will just discuss them at a high level. Here they are:

1. Tasks: Getting the Work Done

Every team exists to do something, right? To complete some set of tasks and/or achieve some sort of goal(s). We always need to keep in mind this question, "What is the work that we're trying to accomplish?"

2. Relationships: Supporting the People

The second critical element that we need to pay attention to is supporting and nurturing the team to create the element of **connectedness**. This isn't about getting the work done; instead, this is about maintaining the people and the relationships on the team. The question to ask here is, "How are we supporting one another?"

A Team's Purpose: Vision, Mission, and Values

At the team level, the lines between vision and mission become somewhat blurred. Why? Because the mission of a team is already defined, at least in part. In other words, every team exists for some reason, for some purpose:

- A pro sports team? Exists to provide entertainment to paying customers
- An information technology team? Exists to provide IT support and expertise to internal/external customers
- A board of directors? Exists to provide high-level strategy and oversight
- An ad hoc task force? Exists to solve a problem

The mission is sort of already included, isn't it? Yes...mostly. We do need to make sure that the mission is clearly defined, both to members of the team and to key external stakeholders of the team (e.g., customers, bosses, etc.). Basically, the mission usually needs to be *refined*, but not necessarily *defined*.

As a result, in contrast to the personal level (PLPS), for teams I find it more effective to start in the middle (with the mission) and work outwards to the vision (what will things look like when the team is functioning at a high level?) and then to the values (what are the operating principles for the team?). The process I describe in Chapter

12 is collaborative and designed for the entire team to participate. Here, though, it may be useful to develop *your own* ideas and thinking.

1. Define the Team Mission

Why Does this Team Exist?

As we outlined above, every team exists to do something, to complete certain tasks or achieve certain goals. What precisely are your team's objectives?

This might seem like an obvious question—and perhaps it is. But humor me. Can you write down all of the things that your team is officially supposed to be doing, either because your bosses have assigned these tasks or because you as the leader recognized some needs and pulled together a team to address them? Here, it might be helpful to make two separate lists: the *official* duties of the team, and the *unofficial* duties of the team. For example,

Official Objectives:

- Hit sales targets
- Respond to customer issues within 24 hours
- Win enough games to make the playoffs

Unofficial Objectives:

- Provide a great experience so people don't leave the company
- Don't ask for more than minimal resources
- Don't rock the boat or make waves in the organization

Do We Even Need to be a Team?

Once you have your lists, ask yourself this question: does my team really even need to be a team? If the defining characteristic of a team (vs. a group of individuals) is the level of interdependence among the people, ask yourself: could we accomplish the same objectives working as a group of loosely connected individuals? You might...and doing so might just solve some of your problems.

For example, I'm a professor in the Management Department. We often refer to ourselves as the Management Team...but are we really a team? Not really. We are really a collection of individuals who are doing our own teaching and research. We sometimes voluntarily collaborate on these tasks, and we also do team up on ad hoc service projects (specific objective and limited duration), but for the most part...we are not a team in the true sense. **Trying to act like we are a team is pointless and probably counterproductive.**

2. Create the Team Vision

Alright, with our mission defined, we have a target. But how do we want to be doing the work? More specifically, what do we want life to be like when our team is at work? Is it:

- A brief morning meeting, followed by individual work time?
- An open work environment where ideas are shared freely and without constraint?
- A team in which lunchtime is sacred, either for:

- Team social interaction?
- Individual respite or errand-running?
- Eating alone at one's desk to catch up on email?

- Lots of good-natured banter, or a pleasant-but-professional atmosphere?
- A team that craves outside recognition, or one that works contentedly behind the scenes?
- A place where decisions are made together, or one where the boss does the thinking?

None of these possibilities are intrinsically any better or worse than the others; they're just different. But what should your team look like?

Here's another way to think about it: if you hired a video team to create a one-day documentary of your ideal team, what would be in the raw footage? If you paid careful attention to what the team members appeared to be doing, thinking, feeling, saying, reacting to, etc.—what would it look like?

And here's yet another way to think about it: what would it look like to see your team absolutely *flourishing*? Not just performing well, not just reasonably content, but *thriving*…and I mean thriving like a Golden Retriever dashing across a field to catch a Frisbee in mid-air?

This is the mental picture to create in your mind's eye, and then solidify by identifying a tangible reminder. Maybe it's a picture you draw. Maybe it's a symbol. I've even had clients search online for pictures that reflect this ideal vision. Whatever your approach, find something that can remind you of the vision you have in mind.

3. Identify the Core Values of the Team

The idea here is very similar to the idea of values in our PLPS: to act as a day-to-day guide for team functioning. This process should ultimately be done collaboratively (and I walk you through how in Chapter 12), but you also want to have your own thinking developed first.

Remember though, team values exist for the good of the team. They help the team to flourish as team members perform the work. If you think about the team accomplishing its mission (doing its work), what value(s) need to be in place? Maybe it's...

- Trust—that willingness to be vulnerable to one another
- Accountability—the willingness to be held to a standard and a deadline
- Flexibility—the ability to reprioritize in light of new information

Further, for each value, we need to give some thought to defining it. In other words, what does it look like when *this particular team* is (or is NOT) living out that value? For example, if a core team value is accountability, then perhaps a description of that value in action is:

- Team members agree in advance on how rewards will be distributed when goals are achieved

An example of not living the value might be:

- Team members who do not meet agreed-upon goals are allowed to continue without intervention or consequence

A final note here: whereas I strongly suggest identifying only two primary values as an individual, for the team, I suggest identifying three core values. Teams and team dynamics are inherently more complex and you may need to articulate more values to deal with the added complexity.

ORGANIZATIONAL LEVEL: BOTTOM-LINE RESULTS

In this final motivation section, let's talk about organizations. I'm going to use the term **bottom-line results** as shorthand for these outcomes that are related to organizational goals. Chances are, your Next Big Challenge is focused on improving one or more things that are important to your organization. At the very least, we need to be aware of how our activities impact the organization's bottom line.

I want to acknowledge that the term **bottom-line results** has a range of connotations associated with it. On one hand, that might be a very good thing as we keep an eye on profitability or other key outcomes. On the other hand, it might have slightly negative connotation by implying that the only thing that is important is making money. Clearly, it's going to mean different things to different people in different situations. Nevertheless, I am going to use the term because it's critical to identify and focus on bottom-line results throughout leadership development.

We need to understand how our investment of time and money in leader development actually impacts the things that are important to our organizations. The failure to show impact on desired results is one of the reasons why leadership training is often viewed with suspicion. Indeed, showing a direct path from leadership training to organizational results is very challenging.

To be effective, leadership training generally needs to:

- be well-received by the participants, and then
- lead to some sort of learning or skill enhancement, and then
- applied on the job, and then
- connected to bottom-line results, and then
- tested to make sure that the impact is not a result of another, external cause not related to the training

That is a tall order! No wonder why we often just hope that training works, instead of actually finding out if it does. Right now, though, I simply want to get a clear picture of your organization's bottom-line results, and more importantly, **what life could be like if you and your colleagues achieved these results**—in other words, this is your **personal vision about what would happen if all bottom-line results were achieved.** This may be different than the organization's vision, mission, or values (see below) because, for most of us, these things are already determined by the organization. They may or may not resonate with us personally, and therefore they vary in their ability to motivate us.

Instead, we need to translate these organizationally-defined criteria into something that has personal meaning for us. Let's take a look at how to do that.

1. List the Bottom-Line Results

Let's make a list of bottom-line results in two broad categories. The first category has to do with organizational performance metrics—key performance indicators (KPIs) for which you are responsible. These can be anything from sales to profitability, to gross margin, to inventory, to people development, to clients served, to widgets produced. In short, whatever it is that you are being evaluated for, list it here.

The second category is focused on your organization's vision, mission, sense of purpose, or perhaps values. List them—what is important to your organization?

Let me pause and acknowledge that, for many organizations, the stated vision, mission, and values are, for all intents and purposes, bullshit. It's something that some focus group came up with years ago, buried it on the website, and made a nice framed picture to hang on the wall in the lobby. Day-to-day, though, they have no real impact. Even worse, sometimes these items are so broad and the lists so long that you could drive a fleet of trucks through them.

I know...I get it...rare is the organization that has a clearly defined purpose and acts according to it. (I work at a university, remember? And universities are notorious for getting input from everyone [which is good] and then creating policies that address every concern that everyone has [which is not so good, because it causes a lack of focus on the most important things]).

Having said that, every organization has a mission and every organization has operative values. Hopefully, they're the ones that are stated and lived out. Every organization is aiming for something, whether it's well thought out and intentional or not. If you need to, make two side-by-side lists: the stated vision, mission, and values, as well as the *real* vision, mission, and values.

2. Imagine What Life Could Be Like

Once you have your list of KPIs and vision/mission/values, create your own 1-2 paragraph vision of what life could be like—for you personally, but also within your organization—if those KPIs were met and those vision/mission/values were fulfilled. Specifically, think about:

- What **freedom** could you (and your organization) experience? What would an abundance of resources allow you to do?
- What personal and collective **wisdom** would it create? What would your organization know and do better than today?
- How would it encourage **connectedness**, both with one another and with other various stakeholders (especially customers)?

This short document can serve as a motivational guide for you as you continue to work on yourself in the context of your overall organization—a true Me1st approach. It can also provide a number of possible ideas for finding your Next Big Challenge.

Before we wrap this part up, I want to have a special word with those of you who are checked out mentally, have one foot out the door already, or simply do not care much very much.

I see you. I hear you. I have been in that situation.

If this is you, I would like to consider the idea that you might still want to focus on these *bottom-line results,* unless there's some sort of moral or ethical reason not to. The reason I say that is if you're already checked out, if you're already thinking about the next thing and taking action towards it—well, wow, you've got a golden opportunity. You are playing with "house money." You can try some things that you wouldn't have tried otherwise and see what happens. This is a wonderful opportunity for you to practice, to dream a bit. Who knows? Maybe you learn something along the way. And if not...well, how much worse can it get? Just some food for thought.

CONCLUDING THOUGHTS

In this chapter, we are starting with the end in mind to create the motivation we will need for the hard work ahead. We begin with the absolute bedrock of our work: finding our purpose as a leader (with vision, mission, and values). We also consider what life would be like with high functioning teams (tasks and people) and thriving organizations (bottom-line results, both KPIs and vision/mission/values).

In the process of finding and spelling out your motivation, you may have found your Next Big Challenge. Awesome! If you are still unsure, that's OK. This is an iterative process, and it is not always clean and linear. The next chapter, Educate and Evaluate, is a bridge between finding the Next Big Challenge and facing it. I encourage you to revisit this chapter as you gain greater clarity in the chapters that follow. Now it's time to move on to understand more about where we are right now, and what we will need to learn.

FROM FINDING TO FACING THE NEXT BIG CHALLENGE: EDUCATE & EVALUATE

THE ME1ST METHOD, STEP 2

"Education consists mainly of what we have unlearned." —MARK TWAIN

With our motivation defined and our clear sense of what we are trying to achieve in place, we now want to focus our attention on our current reality; in other words, where we are right now in our leader journeys. But what should we be looking at? Where do we even start? We know that the ideals we defined in the motivation step aren't our reality yet, so how do we go about getting an accurate read on things?

Perhaps the obvious answer is "get some feedback" or "collect some data"!

Perfect. I'm a scientist. I love data. But what data are worth collecting, and from whom? Remember, *intrinsic* motivation—coming from within us for its own sake—is the best motivator. A close second is *integrated external motivation*—feedback from others that we treat as a gift. Does it follow that the best data is our own self-view, followed by opinions of others as a close second?

The answer is…it depends. Some insights you have about yourself are accurate but somewhat distorted. Some insights that others have about you may also be accurate, but somewhat distorted. Here's the kicker: you—and only you—are responsible for figuring all of this out.

In this chapter, I am going to try to help you in this quest by taking a look at three things. First, as part of the **educate** process, we will look at some foundational knowledge about leadership—things to keep in mind about yourself as a leader. Next, as an example of the type of knowledge we might need to seek out, I will provide you with some research-based know-how about leader identity and how it can change over time. Finally, we will talk about how to create and **evaluate** data in order to get an accurate view of your current reality as a leader.

Let's start by examining some basics about leaders and leadership.

FOUNDATIONAL EDUCATION: WHAT IS LEADERSHIP?

Before we get into developing our own leadership, it's probably a good idea to lay out some basic concepts about leadership.

First, let's define leadership. For me, this is a funny thing because I've been studying leadership, teaching leadership, coaching leaders for the better part of two decades, and I still have yet to hear the definitive definition of leadership. In fact, I like to joke that if you ask *100* people, "What is leadership?" you are going to receive at least *200* responses to that question. It means a little something different to everyone.

Having said that, here is my working definition of leadership: **Leadership is influencing self and others to achieve a goal.** At its gut level, leadership is about making things happen that wouldn't have happened otherwise, or at least wouldn't have happened as quickly or as efficiently as they could. Put another way, it is all about facing the Next Big Challenge.

Second, it is also helpful to make a **distinction between leader and leadership.** A leader is simply a *person* who is embodying a particular role; that is, a set of behaviors that are expected of a leader. Leadership is about the entire *system* of leading, following, and achieving a goal. Think about this for a second. We all have times when we are influencing ourselves and influencing others and are enacting the role of leader, but we also have times where we are reacting to someone else's influence in a follower role. When we talk about leadership, we are not just talking about leaders, but we're talking about leaders, followers, and the situation which those leaders and followers find themselves.

Third, we need to keep in mind is that **leadership doesn't happen in a vacuum.** In other words, this isn't some theoretical pie-in-the-sky set of ideas. All leadership occurs in real situations, in real time and in real space, and with real people. For example, all interactions between leaders and followers happen against the backdrop of a particular culture. Culture, which I like to define as simply 'the way we do things around here,' can refer to an organization's culture, but can also refer to national culture. So, for instance, the way we lead at Apple might look different from the way we lead at IBM, just as the way we lead in the United States is going to look different from the way that we would lead in China. (As an aside, one of the most powerful things we can develop as leaders is Cultural Intelligence (CQ), which is the capability to function and even thrive in multi-cultural situations. As a result, it is one of my favorite areas for training and development.)

Fourth, leadership is based on a series of **interactions between leader and follower(s).** It's kind of like a dance. One partner makes the first step, but the other partner needs to reciprocate. A leader may put forth an idea, a strong suggestion, or even an order. But before that leader's action means anything, the follower needs to decide how to react to it. Accept it without comment? Accept it with a comment? Suggest modifications? Outright ignore it? It's this back-and-forth dynamic that forms the foundation of leadership.

Fifth, **most of what we can control—or at least influence—as leaders may be found within ourselves.** Can we have influence over followers? Of course. Can we sometimes even influence the situation by changing things around us? Of course. But for the most part, the first thing that we should be doing is looking to change ourselves, because this is where we have the greatest leverage. Most leader-follower systems have predictable patterns of behaviors and predictable outcomes. There's a predictable process. When we practice the **Me1st Method**, we lead ourselves first in any system of which we are a part, because that's the point of our greatest leverage. Changing ourselves should be our option of first resort, but very often, it's our option of last resort. Most of the time, we have it completely ass-backward.

Sixth, **while we hope that beginning a development plan will have immediate positive results on our effectiveness, in reality, there is almost always a dip in effectiveness first,** followed by a rebound. If you've ever watched *Sesame Street* on PBS, you know that each episode is sponsored by a particular number and a particular letter. So, if we were going to pick a letter to sponsor leader development, that letter would be the letter *J*. Why? Because the trajectory of leader development looks like the letter J:

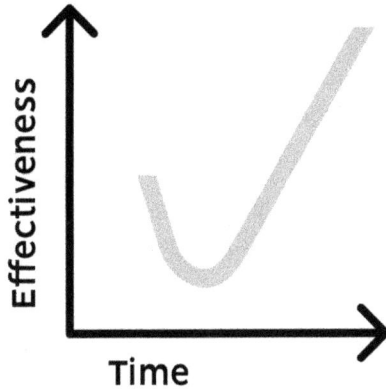

In my experience, this is an accurate description of what we can expect when we begin to develop as leaders, especially when we begin to practice the **Me1st Method** and pursue the Next Big Challenge. There's going to be a lot of resistance. We will have internal resistance as we seek to break old patterns and ways of doing things. We will have external resistance when we are doing something different than we've done before, when we are acting in a way that is different from what people have come to expect from us. They are going to be confused and are likely to double down in their efforts to get us to revert to the way we used to function. Again, I want to emphasize that this isn't a consciously manipulative thing. It is a natural systems-based reaction to us as we seek to lead ourselves first, to assert ourselves, to present our own best thinking, to be more ourselves as an emotionally mature person.

Well, this sounds like fun, doesn't it? "Hey, guess what? If you start developing yourself as a leader, the first results you are going to see are a drop in your effectiveness, or at least your felt effectiveness. It's going to take you a while to even get back to the same level you started with, let alone make much progress!"

OK, so it's not fun—but it really shouldn't surprise us, either. Think about anything that's new and worth doing. There's usually a dip. If you're a couch potato and you decided to run a marathon, those first few times getting off the couch are tough. We're actually going to feel a little bit worse, with much huffing and puffing. Eventually, though, you hit that bottom, and then you're starting to work your way back up. First, you can do three miles comfortably, and pretty soon you can do ten. Then before you know it, several months down the road, you're ready to run a marathon. Leader development works exactly the same way.

To sum up all these introductory points, leadership is about influencing self and others to achieve a goal. It's about getting something to happen that wouldn't have otherwise happened. When we think leadership, we have to keep in mind leader, follower(s), and the situation, as well as the dynamic systemic interplay between those three elements. The key leverage point in all of this is to work on ourselves first. We have the most control over ourselves, so focusing on ourselves first sets us up with the best chance of impacting the system and getting the results that we're seeking.

EDUCATION ABOUT HOW LEADERS DEVELOP: LEADER IDENTITY

In this section, I want to take a deeper look at some research that I believe is enormously helpful for Next Big Challenge leaders for two reasons. First, it is an example of the type of learning that is helpful for Next Big Challenge leaders. Second, and more importantly, this particular topic is the bedrock for ongoing leader development. Identity is simply the answer to two questions, "Who am I?" and "Who do others know me to be?" Leader identity is the answer to very similar questions, "Am I a leader?" and "Do others see me as a leader?"

Why is leader identity important? Well, there's a good deal of research that shows that leader identity forms the foundation for ongoing leader development, and it also impacts who is recognized as a leader. For instance, my colleagues and I did a study that showed that when a person is recognized as a leader by their friends and family members, they take that recognition, internalize it, and actually see themselves as more of a leader at work.[1] In turn, it leads to them displaying more leadership behaviors like setting a vision and inspiring creative thinking. So, leader identity does impact leader actions.

More importantly, though, understanding identity is vital for Next Big Challenge leaders for this reason: **truly big challenges always include identity shifts.** In fact, working on your identity is at the very heart of facing a big challenge.

- Taking on a new role? Your identity is growing.
- A new organization? Your identity is changing.
- A new career? Your identity is going to be different.
- Leading a major change? Your identity needs to evolve.

OK, so how does all of this work? What makes up a leader identity? How does it change? Why is it important? To answer these questions, I'm going to present identity as a few different building blocks.

BUILDING BLOCK 1: IDENTITIES HAVE TWO PARTS

Each person's identity has two major parts: **personal** and **social**.

The first part is your **personal identity**. This refers to the individual, internal characteristics about you as a person: your personality traits, your individual past experiences, or your own internal desire to lead. For example, I am six foot one, so I'm somewhat taller than most people, and I've always enjoyed public speaking. These two characteristics helped me to become recognized as a leader (there's research that shows that physical height and speaking ability are related to leadership recognition).

The second part is your **social identity**. This part has to do with your external, interpersonal characteristics. It is important to note that social identity has two levels. The first level—the *relational level*—has to do with the different relationships that we are a part of. The key phrase for the relational level is "I am, in part because you are." For example, on the day my oldest daughter was born, I became a parent. I immediately became a parent because of the relationship with my daughter. Along with that new relationship, I took on a whole new set of responsibilities. I was recognized by other people as a parent, and more was expected of me. So that relationship impacted my leader identity by conferring upon me rights, roles, and responsibilities that I did not previously have.

The second level of social identity is called the **collective level,** which has to do with the different groups that we're a part of. We're a member of a particular family, we're a citizen of a particular nation, and we're an employee of the organization that we work for, and so on. For example, I'm a professor, and being a member of that profession generally buys me some deference and respect, at some level in some parts of the world. There's a flip side of that, too; some people are kind of skeptical of professors. If I would say, "I'm a professor", they might respond with, "Oh, you're just theoretical. You're living in the ivory tower. You don't know about anything about the way the world really works." So, whether it's respect or a sense of, "I don't know if you know what you're doing", being a member of the group "professors" impacts my leader identity.

Before moving on, I'd like to point out that managing the two parts of one's identity—personal and social—is one of the greatest challenges as a leader. Keeping a balance between being an individual and being part of a relationship or a member of a group is a difficult, life-long challenge. It's another way of looking at the challenge of defining oneself within a system, just as we looked at in Chapter 5.

BUILDING BLOCK 2: YOU ACTUALLY HAVE MULTIPLE IDENTITIES

The technical term for the second building block of leader identity is *sub-identities*, but I think it is easier to just think in terms of having multiple identities to answer the question of "Who am I?"

For example, I'm Mike Palanski. I'm Mike the professor. I'm Mike the coach. I'm Mike the business owner. I'm Mike the husband. I'm Mike the dad. I'm Mike the friend. I'm Mike the over-analyzer. I'm Mike the reluctant Christian. I'm Mike the wannabe world traveler. I'm Mike the barely-running runner.

I'm all of these things, and more. The best way to describe me is as a constellation of multiple identities, but notice that they are not all equally relevant or equally important. In order to think about this notion, it is helpful to have some categories for sorting out all of these various identities.

The first category we will consider is the **active identity.** Think of the active identity as the clothes that you have on right now. That's the part of your identity that you're thinking about and you're acting according to, right now. For example, my "teacher" sub-identity is active right now because I'm writing this chapter, but a little bit later on today, my "amateur recreational athlete" sub-identity will be active when I go skiing.

The second category is called the **provisional identity.** In this category, we are "trying on" various identities to see if they "fit" and see if we want to keep them. Actually, this category includes thinking about *possible* identities ("what would it be like if I ____?"). For example, last year I had a couple of home improvement projects and I thought about being the guy who would replace the flooring and being the guy who would replace the sink. In order to turn these thoughts into some sort of tangible action (a provisional identity), I did a little bit with the sink, and before you know it, I had switched out the vanity and replaced the sink and I felt pretty good. That provisional identity kind of stuck. On the other hand, I was less confident about replacing flooring, so I decided to do a very small section. And after I did that very small section, I was drained. It was too much work, and it looked like hell. So I picked up the phone and called my friend who's a flooring guy, and hired him.

The third category is called the **discarded identity.** A discarded identity is something that used to be part of us but isn't any longer. Here's another example, and although not directly related to leadership, hopefully, it makes the point. I grew up as a Pittsburgh Pirates fan baseball fan. But when I became a young adult, my wife and I moved to St. Louis for five years. If you've ever been to St. Louis or lived in St. Louis, you know that the St. Louis Cardinals are the heart and soul of St. Louis. As they like to say, it's definitely a baseball town. After living there for a few years, I slowly started to develop an affinity for the Cardinals. And for a while, I was kind of rooting for both teams. But finally, my love for the Cardinals grew so strong that I quit rooting for the Pirates. I discarded my identity as a Pittsburgh Pirates fan.

For Next Big Challenge leaders, understanding multiple identities can be a goldmine. Think about this for a second: one way to think about facing big challenges is as a process of trying new things (which, by the way, is the last step of the **Me1st Method**) and taking on *provisional identities* and deciding whether to keep them or discard them. For example, maybe you have never had the responsibility to interact with external investors, but your new role demands this skill. A great way to begin to build the skill is by *provisionally* taking on the sub-identity of "investor whisperer." Maybe you find that it is working and you keep it as a ready-to-become-active-when-needed-identity. And maybe you find that it doesn't work, so you discard it and try something else (perhaps the "just-the-facts investor relations person" or something).

Makes sense, right? Well, there is a predicable process for how this happens—and this brings us to our next building block.

BUILDING BLOCK 3: PHASES OF IDENTITY SHIFT

This might be the most important insight in this entire chapter for Next Big Challenge leaders. When we are facing a big challenge, our identity is put to the test, often in new and difficult ways. We will often feel anxious, threatened, and conflicted. These feelings are perfectly normal; in fact, experiencing them is likely a sign that you are on the right track. Let's unpack the phases of identity shift.

The first phase is known as **separation,** and it is marked by the challenge of losing an existing identity. For example, suppose you are an expert individual contributor who has a great deal of autonomy in the kinds of work you do and choosing the people you work with. You are now being offered a formal leadership role. You are excited about its possibilities, but you fear that you will miss being the autonomous expert. Similarly, as we begin to search for the Next Big Challenge, we may begin to feel a sense of loss for what once was—the sense of comfort and familiarity that is left over from our previous big challenge.

I like to call the second phase simply **in-between.** In this phase, you acutely feel the challenge of moving between identities. People in this phase often describe it as "being in limbo" or "being neither here nor there." This phase might be marked by tension or even fear of trying to take on a new identity that is not valued by others (e.g., members of your organization, or perhaps your family) or is not consistent with others' expectations. For example, perhaps you are beginning a new side hustle that you hope might become a full-time career. Maybe you want to be a yoga instructor, but it isn't yet clear how that role can coincide with your day job as a stock trader. You find that your new yoga friends aren't quite sure about their new stock-trading colleague, and your broker friends look at you like you have three heads for doing yoga. And your family is sending all sorts of mixed messages about this shift. The phase is definitely about facing the Next Big Challenge.

The third phase is **integration.** In this phase, you have solidified your new identity (to continue our two prior examples, perhaps as a formal leader or as a yoga instructor). Now, your challenge is to figure out how this new identity fits together with your other identities. For example, perhaps you are trying to reconcile being an engaged parent with your new role of formal leader, or being an analytic stock trader with being a mindful yoga instructor. You are now embracing the Next Big Challenge in your very identity.

BUILDING BLOCK 4: INTEGRATED IDENTITY AS A LEADER

Interestingly, being a leader—your leader identity—may help to resolve issues of integration.

Leader identity is unique in that it can serve as a way to integrate many of our other identities. Think about it: you can be a leader at work, certainly, but you can also be a leader at home. You can be a leader in the community with volunteers, or you can lead your book club. You can be a leader as a parent, but you can also act as a leader for aging parents. We do things in each of these roles that reflect who we are as a leader. Many times, we don't even recognize what we are doing is in fact leadership until someone points it out to us; nevertheless, it is leading.

As a Next Big Challenge leader, this way of thinking about identity is incredibly powerful. As you face your Next Big Challenge—whatever it may be—you still are keeping and growing your **leader identity.** You are a leader no matter where you go or what you do. Your leader identity provides a sense of stability and coherence even as your circumstances change.

LEADER IDENTITY AND THE ME1ST METHOD

When we commit to following the **Me1st Method** of leader development, we are inescapably committing to working on our own identity. Having a well-defined sense of self and developing emotional maturity means having a strong identity. Being a vital and vibrant part of social systems means having a strong identity. Being a life-long learner means having a strong identity.

In fact, people with a strong leader identity tend to do three things. First, they **actively seek development.** They're more likely to be taking classes, training, seeking out mentors, reading books, or listening to podcasts—basically anything they can get their hands on to improve. The second thing they do is **put themselves purposefully into new and uncomfortable situations in order to learn.** They want to be challenged. They want to be stretched. They want to face the unfamiliar. As a leader, they want to see if they can work through it, grow themselves, and then show others how to do it. Sound familiar, dear Next Big Challenge leader?

The final thing they do is **actively search for and recognize hidden leadership development opportunities**. They notice the unnoticed, little things where they can develop as a leader, and they learn leadership lessons almost anywhere in any situation.

Here's one final thought: leader identity is also the foundation for more visible aspects of leading. It informs what leaders do, how leaders think, and how leaders feel. You can relate it to just about any other leadership topic that you study.

EVALUATE YOURSELF: ASSESSING YOUR CURRENT STATE

Having begun to educate ourselves about leadership, we would do well to understand our current status as a leader. Here's how:

THE PROCESS

First, let's break down each of the parts of those three motivational documents. For the PLPS, divide the vision, the mission, and the values. For your team outcomes, list each part of the mission, the vision, and the values separately. Likewise, break out the bottom-line organizational results. Now, for each one of those, give some thought to your current situation.

- Describe, in as much detail as you can, the current situation. If you have other forms of data (e.g., sales figures), include them.
- If you feel comfortable doing so, share your observations with others who are familiar with the situations. Ask them to comment on the accuracy of your observations, and to add their own.

- List the ways that the current situation reflects the desired future state you have specified. Even if these are very small ways, list them. Start with strengths.
- Also list the ways in which the current situation needs to change to become your desired future.

Sounds simple enough, right? That's basically what all leadership assessments (surveys and the like) do. Sometimes we need to conduct more sophisticated data gathering, but very often we just need to slow down and try to paint an accurate picture.

A POSSIBLE FAST FORWARD: 360 SURVEYS AND OTHER LEADERSHIP ASSESSMENTS

I try to limit my advice-giving activities to subjects where I really do know what I am talking about. This is one of those subjects.

Assessments that ask you questions and then provide feedback can be helpful. Assessments that ask others about you and then provide feedback to you can be even more helpful. As we mentioned back in Chapter 1, the results from a 360-degree survey helped Sam the engineer to develop the insight he needed to really grow as a leader. (As a reminder, a 360-degree survey compares a leader's self-perceptions to the perceptions of those that know the leader well [boss, peers, direct reports, but possibly also family and friends]. The resulting analysis can provide insight and actionable feedback to the leader.)

I have been designing, implementing, and debriefing 360 surveys for over a decade. My colleagues and I created a research-based 360 that we've used with over 400 leaders and thousands of raters. I've seen it all, and I've come to this conclusion: 360s rarely live up to their promise. Here's why:

1. **Measuring perceptions instead of reality**: 360s are supposed to measure observable behaviors, but they typically actually measure others' perceptions of those behaviors (even when the questions are written well). Even when people have not actually observed the behaviors in question, they answer *as if* they have firsthand knowledge. People don't like to be without an answer, so they guess—even if they are provided an option called something like "I don't know" or "not applicable".

2. **Over-reliance on quantitative data:** I have helped to create 360 datasets with tens of thousands of data points. Let me tell you: there's not much actionable information there. The questions and competencies tend to be very highly correlated, which doesn't provide much helpful feedback to the leaders. However, all of the charts, graphs, and numbers make it *feel like* there is substance there. More often than not, it's a mirage.

3. **Reliance on anonymity**: 360s are designed to protect raters' anonymity. Makes sense, right? If people are anonymous, they will be more likely to give honest feedback. However, providing anonymity actually promotes irresponsible behaviors and ends up undermining the developmental purpose of the 360 itself. To put it bluntly: if your people are concerned about attaching their names to their feedback, then you have much bigger issues to deal with—issues like fostering trust and psychological safety. Further, there is research to suggest that anonymous comments tend to be more negative in tone for women (vs. men).

4. **Poor implementation:** 360s are often never actually used for ongoing development; what's worse, they are sometimes used for performance evaluation of leaders. Both of these practices undermine the purpose of the 360s. So if you have

observations (data) from others, make sure it is given with development in mind; otherwise, the data may be skewed.

5. **Limited usefulness**: In reality, 360 feedback rarely provides new insight to leaders. They might find little nuggets of wisdom, but there is rarely a career-changing impact. Of the hundreds of 360 results that I've debriefed with leaders, I'd estimate that maybe 10% find game-changing insight (like Sam did). The other 90% find confirmation of what they already knew or at least suspected.

6. **Questions and models are too generic**: Generic 360 questions—even ones that are research-validated—lead to generic feedback. They rarely provide leaders with actionable ideas that fit their unique situation. Thoughtful leaders and talent development professionals already have a good sense of the "top ten things effective leaders do", so why are we wasting time and effort focusing on them? As we mentioned early in this chapter, leadership does not occur in a made-up vacuum.

I know this all sounds pretty pessimistic. My colleagues and I are working on a new version of a 360 that can overcome some of these limitations. In the meantime, though, here's my best advice: be careful. Specifically:

- **Look at the content of the questions carefully**

Off-the-shelf surveys will ask generic questions (e.g., "How often does this person talk enthusiastically about the future?") That might be OK, but it makes it more difficult for the people completing the survey to answer—and it makes the results harder to interpret (for example, talks enthusiastically...about what, exactly?). It is MUCH better to have questions that ask about specific topics (e.g., "How often does this person talk about the new Whizbang Cereal Varnish campaign?")

- **Look at the wording of the questions carefully**

Generally, good questions will describe a specific behavior and ask how often you engage in it. For example, a fairly strong question would be, "How often does this leader ask open-ended questions?" with a scale ranging from 1 (never) to 5 (frequently, if not always). An even better format would be to follow up that question with one like this: "Please describe the most recent time when this leader asked an open-ended question." If the person taking the survey is unable to think of a specific instance, then that person's score of 4 of 5 probably is not accurate.

- **Look at the quantitative data carefully**

First, look at the mean (average) scores. If they are all very similar to one another, it might indicate a problem with the format. Second, look at the variation for each question (often given as a Standard Deviation score, or perhaps represented visually with "whiskers" on top of a bar graph). A moderate amount of variation is probably a good sign. Very low or very high variation may be a sign that the data have limited accuracy.

In my experience, a thoughtful accounting of your own current state that you discuss with 2-3 trusted, honest, and knowledgeable other people is probably a good choice for most people.

CONCLUDING THOUGHTS

In this chapter, we looked at some foundational knowledge about leadership. We also took a deep look at leader identity. Finally, we discussed how to gather or create data about your current situation (including a closer look at assessments).

To wrap up, I want to point out something important. Most leadership training focuses, in one way or another, on knowledge or skill acquisition—in other words, education. These are important—but without the rest of the framework, they are also limited. We need to know why we are getting knowledge or skills (motivate). We need to have some idea of what to do with them (strategize). And we need to have a way to put them into practice (test).

Chapter 7 ½

Note from Mike: This little section is basically the Pluto of this book. Is it a chapter? A dwarf chapter? A bunch of words? What do we do with it? I don't know...so I just decided to park it right here. Here you go...

The 1 Thing at a Time Concept—and a Funny but Insightful Story

> *"The one thing I learned was how much I didn't know"*
> – WILLIAM PALUMBO

This isn't a chapter, really. It's a really short reflection with one little message: keep going!

THE 1 THING AT A TIME CONCEPT

As we head into the final two elements (Strategize and Test), the reality of the difficulties and dangers of leadership will become more real, more apparent. The list of things you feel you need to work on may actually grow as you gain a greater sense of what is needed.

That's a good thing because becoming a better leader is a lifelong process. Whatever big challenge you are currently facing, I can guarantee this: it won't be your last.

Take a deep breath and realize that you *do not* need to (and—frankly —*should not* and *cannot*) tackle everything at once. It's perfectly OK to make note of things for now and keep focused on the task at hand. When I am facilitating teams, we have a flipchart or board off to the side of the room called "Parking Lot" to make note of things that come up which are important but should not be addressed immediately.

Make your own Parking Lot.

And keep focused on 1 thing at a time.

A FUNNY BUT INSIGHTFUL STORY

The quote above is from Mr. Palumbo, my 10th grade driver's ed and 11th grade world cultures teacher. A bald man with thick glasses, he was the high school version of an absent-minded professor with the apt nickname of Uncle Bumby. In fact, he was so absent-minded that students would sometimes answer essay questions about Chinese culture or driving in snow by listing what they ate for breakfast somewhere in the essay, just to see if he'd notice.

He usually didn't.

One day, we were doing some individual work in class while he was grading papers. At one point, he beckoned to me, "Hey Palanski. Come up here a second." As I approached his desk, he pointed to the paper he was grading. "Look at this. One of your classmates answered my question about Chinese culture with 'pancakes, bacon, and orange juice.' Students have been doing this for a while, because they think I don't notice. But the truth is that I just don't care."

Boom! Mic drop!

Turns out the whole Uncle Bumby bit was a façade. That old fox knew exactly what was going on.

By the way, good 'ole Uncle Bumby wasn't checked out. He was quirky for sure, but the students loved him and learned from him. When he preached the virtue of pulling over to let an aggressive tailgater pass safely in driver's ed, he actually lived it out (seriously—my friend John saw him do it, right there on Engle Road).

Mr. Palumbo was focused on displaying and living his own best thinking while remaining connected to others instead of "performing." That's what we Next Big Challenge leaders are striving for, too.

Since we are roughly mid-book, let me remind you that help is available:

Me1stMethod.com

One thing at a time. Let's keep going.

8

A PLAN FOR FACING THE NEXT BIG CHALLENGE: STRATEGIZE

THE ME1ST METHOD, STEP 3

"Tactics without strategy is simply the noise before defeat" —SUN TZU

So far, we've spent a good deal of effort generating motivation by painting our ideal picture for ourselves, our teams, and our organizations. We have also taken the time to educate ourselves about the most important parts of leader development and to evaluate our current situation. Now it's time to start pulling these pieces together in order to get ready for action. It's time to create a strategy. And we are going to do that in four steps.

First of all, we're going to do a gap analysis (or, for a little panache, we could call it "minding the gap", just like getting on The Tube in London). Next, we are going to create a preliminary plan, followed by ideation about how to execute that plan. Finally, we are going to focus on a few high-leverage opportunities. By the way, notice that we are implementing both the third discovery from Intentional Change Theory, as well as the third form of Multiple Intelligences, metacognition.

MIND THE GAP

We first want to get an accurate sense of where we are and compare it to where we want to be. Let's start by taking another look at the three parts for motivation: our personal leadership purpose statement, our team high-performance conditions, and our organizational bottom-line results. Remember, these are what we're shooting for; all of these represent our desired end state.

We are getting ready to face our Next Big Challenge, but we also want to set the stage to embrace it, too. We intentionally put our motivational work aside for a time, so let's pause to reflect. Does it still resonate? Does anything need to be tweaked? If so, please do that now, especially with your Personal Leadership Purpose Statement. Remember, this is an iterative, back-and-forth process.

Once we are satisfied with our desired outcomes, let's take another look at our current state from Chapter 7—where we are today.

Compare the two. The goal for this step is to create a clear picture of the gap that exists between what you desire and what you have. At this point, don't worry about the distance between them, or try to figure out a path between them. We will get to those steps. For now, just aim for accuracy.

It's kind of like you're standing on one mountain top looking over at the next mountain top. You're thinking, "I just want to get over there." But what you don't see clearly are all of the boulders and the rocks and the streams and the trees and the little ridges that you need to work through to get to the other mountain top. That's fine. For now, we're just focusing on where we are and where we want to go. We are just obtaining an accurate picture of the gap between the two.

MAKE SOME LISTS

In this step, we want to sketch some rough ideas about what we need to do to get from where we are now to where do we desire to go. To do this, I'd like to suggest that we make two lists. The first is a list of the skills, capabilities, resources, relationships, mindsets, knowledge, and time we might need—basically, a list of anything that we think can help us.

Here's a helpful hack: use the results of your work from Chapter 7 and any supplemental work you've done to guide your thinking. What do you need to grow or change your identity? Do you need skills related to doing tasks, supporting people, or driving change? Do you need to develop your thinking, or work on expanding your emotional maturity?

The second list is a list of things you might need to get rid of. Ask yourself: what do I have now that is not serving me, that's actually holding me back, keeping me down, or just distracting me? Are there projects that I'm working on right now that are not helpful in getting me to where I really want to be? Are there some past problems that I need to take care of or relationships I need to mend? Are there relationships I need to put on the back burner, or perhaps end altogether?

In short, we are assessing what we need to say *yes* to, and what we need to say *no* to, in order to focus on the most important things. I appreciate that this process can be very challenging. There can be a huge emotional component. If we are serious about it, it will impact our very identity. Being a Next Big Challenge leader is not easy. Let's continue to acknowledge that.

IDEATE

So far, we've identified our gaps and created our lists of things to acquire and things to let go. Now let's start thinking of some possible ways of closing the gap by working our lists. I'm suggesting four ways to think of ideas here—but really, feel free to generate ideas any way you can.

1. **Direct Experience.** Think of some ways to give yourself some direct experience with whatever is on your list. What we are looking for here is a small, quick win that will give us even just a little bit of relevant experience. For example, perhaps you have identified developing public speaking skills as important for you. Your ultimate goal might be delivering a one-hour keynote speech, but could you start with doing a short presentation for your local library? Or perhaps you have realized that you need to set appropriate boundaries with your boss, but you are fearful about doing so. Could you perhaps start by being more assertive about setting a personal boundary, like saying that you are actually not going to host everyone for that stupid National Donut Day breakfast that your cousin assigned to you? (By the way, I realize that for some of you setting a boundary with your boss would be way, way easier than setting a boundary about hosting a family gathering.)

2. **Connect with Others.** Identify others who have done what you want to do, and try to connect with them. Are there mentors that you can seek out who've already done what you desire to do? Are there support groups? Are there like-minded peers? We want to see that someone else is doing what we'd decide to do, both to learn how they're doing it, but also to give us a sense of confidence that we could do this too. By the way, my friend Kristin and her colleagues have developed a powerful method to analyze and grow your professional network. Check it out in the workbook.

3. **Make a Case.** We can also use our left brain and make a very rational argument for why we need to do something. The goal is to create a well-reasoned and well-informed case for ourselves that we can use to remind us of how we are set up for success. To be sure, a rational case is not enough by itself, but it can be very powerful in those moments where our emotions are flooding us, either positively or negatively.

4. **Psych ourselves up.** We can also give ourselves a power boost by psyching ourselves up. Are there strategies that we can use that will give us a short-term boost to perform better? Let's marshal those resources as well. Do you have a favorite music playlist that you listen to? Do you have a picture on your bathroom mirror of your family, or that dream house, or the way the world will be? Plan for ways to give yourself a lift when you need it.

FOCUS, FOCUS, FOCUS

If you completed the three preceding steps, you might be feeling both excited and discouraged at the same time. Excited, because you have some good ideas. Discouraged, because the gap just seems wider than it ever has. You might be thinking that there are just so many things that you need to acquire and so many things you need to get rid of. It can be really overwhelming.

Let's reign that in. Here's a great little exercise to help. I call it the **Five Sixes.** Here's how it works:

- First, think about something you can do in the next **6 minutes.** What is one tangible thing you can accomplish right now to begin to close the gap? Perhaps it is firing off a quick email to set up a meeting for the conversation you've been avoiding. Or maybe it is as simple as creating a note to put on your mirror or monitor to remind yourself of a behavior you want to do ("Ask a Question") or an identity you want to try on ("I am a Leader").

- Second, think of something you can accomplish in the **next 6 hours**. What is something you can do today? Could you perhaps search for an article to read? Could you take a walk while listening to a podcast? Could you carve out 15 minutes to journal and self-reflect?

- Third, I want you to think of one thing that you could do in the next **6 days**. So in less than a week, what is something that you could pursue? This short timeframe helps us to create action and perhaps see some results (whether positive or negative). Perhaps, like Nancy (the nurse manager whom we met back in Chapter 1), it's creating a micro-habit like asking others what else they have done to solve their own problem before jumping in with the answer or advice.

- Fourth, let's think about something you can accomplish in the next **6 weeks**. Six weeks is an ideal timeframe for trying something that requires an investment of time and treasure but is not likely to give immediate feedback or results. It's long enough to gain some momentum, but not so long that you feel as if you've wasted time and resources if it is not working out. For example, perhaps you've been contemplating holding "office hours" every day from 1-2 PM; in other words, blocking a time when you will be available to handle any off-the-cuff concerns from others. Six weeks is sufficient to get a sense of whether this practice works well for you, and for your team.

- Finally, let's also pick out one item to focus on for the next **6 months**. This timeframe is especially useful for activities that require some sort of outside assistance. It's a perfect timeframe for working with a coach or obtaining training (like the Me1st Academy) or completing a substantial project.

GOAL SETTING VS. GROWTH LETTING

Before we conclude this chapter, I'd like to offer one more thing for your consideration. You've just created a list of five to-do items. The logical thing to do would be to frame each of those action items as a goal.

That might be a good thing to do, but not necessarily. Hear me out. Goals are helpful, especially for developing skills. Sometimes, though, we need to simply begin in a general direction without a specific destination in mind. With these two thoughts in mind, let me talk about the difference between **goal setting** and **growth letting.**

1. Goal Setting

Based on research begun by Edwin Locke and Gary Latham[1], goal setting theory is perhaps the most studied, best-validated area in all of organizational science. Study after study has demonstrated that having specific and difficult-but-achievable goals along with some sort of reliable feedback mechanism will increase performance. Thus, the SMART (specific, measurable, achievable, realistic, time-bound) goal has rightly become a staple of modern management techniques for both individuals and organizations.

If we have a clear goal, it is a pretty straightforward process to see if we have met the goal or not, so that narrows down our possible outcomes by half. But suppose we did hit our goal. Does that tell us whether this was the most appropriate goal (strategy item) to pursue?

No, it really does not. The goal-setting approach, while powerful, is incomplete.

There's another problem here: setting goals may actually *inhibit* leader development. Goal setting is terrific for driving incremental behavior change or learning a new skill for routine tasks. Thus, goals are perfect for doing things like becoming better at keeping a meeting on its time schedule, or learning to golf better. It might even be good at facilitating important actions—like setting a goal to touch base with every team member at least twice a week.

Even in situations in which they are useful, however, goals activate what psychologists call a **performance orientation**—that is, our focus is on "not failing" and/or "demonstrating our competence" to others. This approach is not always so desirable in developmental situations; we need another way of growing, too.

2. Growth Letting

Growth letting? Yes, as in "Are you going to let yourself grow?"

The process of growing as a leader—that is, living out our purpose as a leader (putting values into action to live out our mission in support of our vision)—is novel, complex, and adaptive; in other words, it's messy. In growth letting, we can try nearly anything as long as we keep one simple question in mind: Is this activity moving me closer to or further away from fulfilling my purpose?

The growth letting approach activates what psychologists call a **learning (or growth) orientation**—that is, the focus is on improvement, and there is less concern about failure or proving one's competence.

How does it work? One excellent way is through a process of sensemaking, which involves four overlapping steps:

1. **Noticing.** We pay careful attention to what is happening (or not happening). We try to take in as many details as we can about the situation. For example, let's say our strategy item is focused on becoming more comfortable and effective in speaking up in meetings.

In the noticing step, we would pay attention to opportunities that might arise, how we react to them, what we are feeling, what others are doing, and so on.

2. **Interpreting.** In this step, we are going to attach some sort of meaning to what we are observing. This meaning can be provisional and open to change, but we want to start somewhere. For example, if we notice that we are feeling nervous about speaking up, we might attribute it to a fear of not knowing enough to say something useful.

3. **Authoring.** Next, we are going to create a mini-plan for action. In other words, we answer the question, "How am I going to react to what I am noticing?" To continue our example, we might think, "I am going to say something at the next opportunity. I will then look for reactions from others, as well as try to objectively evaluate what I have said myself."

4. **Enacting:** In this final step, we actually put our mini-plan into action, and we see what happens (we go back to the Noticing step again). In our example, I might offer an opinion. I do not see any visible reaction from anyone, but I notice I feel better for just speaking up.

When we are mindful of this sensemaking process, we have a way to try new things and learn from them, without being overly concerned with the results. As Next Big Challenge leaders, we often do not fully know what we are heading towards. Even if we do have a sense of the final destination, the path towards it isn't always clear. Having a mix of goal setting and growth letting is desirable.

Do one final thing before we move on. Take one more look at your list of Five Sixes. See if you can frame at least one of them as a goal (hint: it's often the 6-minute, 6-hour, or 6-day item) and at least one as a growth letting item (hint: it's often the 6-week or 6-month item). Allow yourself to do both.

OK! We are now ready to take our final step: Test.

9

FACING AND EMBRACING THE NEXT BIG CHALLENGE: TEST

THE ME1ST METHOD, STEP 4

"Good tests kill flawed theories; we remain alive to guess again."—KARL POPPER

We have arrived at the action phase of the **Me1st Method**! It's time to try something, to experiment until we get to the point where we can embrace our Next Big Challenge. To do that, we're going to look at four things: the mad scientist mindset, running a great experiment, analyzing the data, and then taking action. And for these four things, I want to draw on my own experience as a social scientist. You see, the biggest part of my career as a professor is being a leadership researcher, and being a sound researcher means running scientific experiments from time to time. So I'm going to use that as our jumping-off point because **good leaders are also good scientists**. That's the mindset that we want to use. Let's do some science!

DEVELOPING THE MAD SCIENTIST MINDSET

What does a mad scientist mindset look like? Well, first of all, just to get into the mood, please take a moment and close your eyes (OK, OK —actually finish this paragraph and then close your eyes). Picture yourself in a Frankenstein-type lab with a bunch of boiling liquids and beakers and tubes and arching electricity. And of course, you should be wearing a lab coat and goggles. Can you picture it? Good. Now let's go crazy. Let's go all in with this mad scientist experiment thing. Find or create some sort of a reminder for yourself that you are a scientist. Maybe it's an actual lab coat, a little lab coat you found on Etsy, or a pair of goggles. Something to remind yourself that:

I. Am. A. Scientist.

Why are we going all in on this mad scientist theme? We want to engage our learning mindset, and getting into the specifics will help us do just that. We're not beholden to the results here, so this mindset is going to allow us to try things that we might not have tried otherwise. **We're not primarily concerned about the results; instead, we are much more concerned with the process and the details.**

As scientists, we practice the scientific method. We have an idea. We do some background research. We come up with a hypothesis, we design an experiment, and we test. We get some data and we analyze the data. And whether it comes out the way we thought it would or not, we've learned something. As mad scientists, we are trying to learn something. Sometimes we get it right, but many times we don't.

All right? Developing the mindset is the first part of becoming a mad scientist. The next part is focusing on the details.

FOCUSING ON THE DETAILS

As scientists, we need to be laser-focused on the details. Even if you're not a detail-oriented person, this is one place where you want to do your best. And, by the way, I fit myself into this category. Believe it or not, I am a big-picture person. I like to think about big concepts and how they fit together. Honestly, it takes a lot of effort and practice for me to do a deep dive into details. I can do it when needed, but it doesn't come naturally.

I'll give you a quick example, something outside of the realm of what we're doing here. Every time I've bought or sold a home, I have carried around a little notebook with me. In that notebook, I make detailed notes about everything: every conversation with real estate agents and attorneys and home inspectors—anybody involved in the process. I have information there about interest rates, deadlines, and local laws. So when things go wrong (and they are bound to at some point), I can whip out the little notebook, flip to the right page, and be like, "No, no, no. Here's what you said on December 6th." Those details have saved me a lot of aggravation when issues arise. It's not something I do day in and day out, but when needed, I can do it.

I want to suggest that this time of growth is one of those times where we want to flex that detail muscle to the extent that we can. Look, there is a lot of help out there. A lot of help. There are apps, and there are free or inexpensive training courses that can help us get to that level of detail. We do not need to get too sophisticated. A simple journal and a calendar that you actually use are sufficient.

So what kinds of details are we focusing on? Keep reading to find out.

MIKE PALANSKI, PH.D.

DESIGNING A GREAT EXPERIMENT

The second thing that we want to do to test is to actually design a great experiment. Here I'm drawing from my training and my almost two decades of experience as a social scientist.

In an experiment, we're basically trying to understand if A causes B. That's it—does A cause B? Here's a very simple example: If I take a baseball and throw it at a window, will the window break? A is me throwing the baseball, and B is the window breaking. Are there other things that can cause a window to break? Absolutely. But what I'm interested in is figuring out if me throwing the baseball at the window is the thing that causes the window to break.

Here's a more leadership-focused example. I'm the leader and I'm having a one-on-one with one of my direct reports. My habit previously has been to jump in and solve whatever problem that person presents. I recognize that this habit is not very helpful, and I want to create an experiment to see if something else might work better. One of the things that I have brainstormed is this: anytime I'm tempted to jump in and solve the problem, instead what I'm going to do is to ask a question and then remain silent.

My experiment setup is this: is A going to lead to B? In this case, is me asking my direct report a question and me remaining silent going to lead to my direct report coming up with an idea about how to solve their own problem? That is what I'm looking for: will my 'A' actions (asking a question, then being silent) lead to their 'B' actions (solving their own problem).

In order for me to design an experiment around this notion, I have to satisfy three different criteria. **Focusing on these three conditions is what separates science from guessing.** These are the three secret ingredients of an experiment.

128

1. A and B need to be correlated

If it's been a while since you studied statistics, remember that a correlation is when some change in the level of A is related to some change in the level of B. For example, if I have a full tank of gas in my car, I can drive for about 5 hours, but if I only have a gallon of gas left, I might only be able to drive for half an hour. The amount of fuel I have is correlated with the time I can spend driving. Returning to our leadership example, there needs to be a correlation between me asking that question and shutting up (A) and my direct report coming up with their own ideas (B).

2. A needs to occur before B

The second part of a good experiment is ensuring that A occurs before B; otherwise, we cannot claim that A causes B. For example, if we have this one-on-one meeting and your direct report walks in says, "Hey, good morning. We have an issue with productivity, but I've come up with this great idea to solve this problem." And then you say, "So what does that mean for you?" followed by silence.

Guess what? We've got B! We've got the result that we wanted: the direct report has come up with their own idea! But it didn't really have anything to do with our actions, did it? It wouldn't make any sense for us to say that our actions (asking that question and then remaining silent) caused that person to come up with their own idea. Only if our actions precede the actions of the other can we infer that our actions caused the other person's actions. A has to occur before B.

3. Eliminate other plausible explanations

To the extent possible, we want to rule out other possible reasons why B might occur. Ideally, we want to eliminate them, but if we can't eliminate them altogether, then we at least want to account for them.

Going back to our example, let's say that both my direct report and I just went to some sort of a leadership training course. One of the things that the trainer was talking about was the need for people to come up with their own ideas about how to solve problems. One of the ways to do that is for leaders to encourage that thinking is by asking a question and then shutting up.

The next day you have this one-on-one meeting, and you are now going to put this idea into action. Your direct report walks in, explains the problem, and then you ask a question and then remain silent. And...presto! The direct report comes up with their own idea.

That's great! A has led to B!

But is the reason why that person thought of that idea because you, the leader, asked the question and then shut up, or is it because you all went to this training and that your direct report was already thinking about, "Hmm, I know how this is going to unfold. I want to go in and be ready with a solution because I'm pretty sure my boss is going to ask me a question and then shut up?" You're both kind of primed to know how this is going to go down.

This is not a good experiment, because you have this other thing (i.e., you both went to the training) and this common experience might be the reason that this meeting unfolded the way that it did.

Ultimately, that's not a bad thing. That's a great benefit of training. That's wonderful. You're making a step towards what you ought to be doing, but we really want to know if asking a question and then remaining silent is something that we can use in any situation. Is it something we can rely on when our direct reports are not expecting it?

So what do we do? Well, we have a few options. First, we could eliminate this problem altogether by attempting to use this technique with a direct report who did not attend the training and is not expecting it. Or we could mitigate the impact by trying it a month after the training (instead of the day after), with the idea that it has faded from memory and the direct report might not be thinking about it.

There are many things we can try, but the most important thing is to recognize the presence of other possible causes of B happening and try to eliminate or control for them.

ANALYZING THE DATA

The next thing that we need to do is to analyze our data. One question we want to answer is: how much of an impact did our experiment have? In our example, did that person come up with an idea? If so, what was the quality of the idea? Did the idea have a better implementation?

Another question we might want to answer is: what secondary impacts did it have? Maybe my direct report's idea was about the same quality as the one I'd offer, but at least it freed me up from having to spend time thinking about it. In this case, it's a win because I've not had to expend resources, and it helped the direct report to develop their own skills. Maybe if we do this again and again and again, it will become an even better idea.

Sometimes we have hard, quantitative data to analyze, but very often in leadership situations, our data can be much more qualitative. In our example, let's say that A did not impact B. Let's say that you asked that question, and kept your mouth shut. In response, the person just sat there completely befuddled.

Now we want to ask ourselves: why did this not work? Is there something that was missing? Is there something else we need to do in this case? This will lead to our next experiment. We might say, "Hmm, maybe this person needs a little bit of training on how to solve their own problem. Or maybe I just need to switch into coach mode a little bit." So you give them a little bit of training, or you coach them, and then you run that experiment again.

Remember, whether the experiment works or not, the idea is to get the best possible data and then to start the process over, either to find something that works, or works better.

TAKING ACTION

Our fourth and final step is short. It's more of a reminder, really. We need to take action by practicing what we have learned. Our newfound wisdom has become part of our leadership repertoire. We want to continue to practice it in new situations and with new people. So— just use it.

CODA: EMBRACING THE NEXT BIG CHALLENGE

The **Me1st Method** has (hopefully) provided you with the guidance to find and face that Next Big Challenge. But what does it look like to actually embrace it? Here a few thoughts:

First, **we might consider how the Me1st Method is an ongoing cycle**. Look at how the overall results of the **Me1st Method** its various parts: motivate, educate and evaluate, strategize, or testing. We want to keep the big picture in mind. It doesn't mean we need to change everything every time we do something new—but we might want to tweak things. Maybe our vision needs to be slightly altered, or maybe we notice an important bottom-line result we overlooked. Perhaps we realize that there are other skills we need to acquire, or we see a more effective strategy. Or maybe we are ready to try another experiment. As we become comfortable with this iterative process, we more readily embrace the challenge.

Second, **we might think about embracing the challenge from a leader identity perspective**, as we learned about in Chapter 7. If the challenge is truly of the Next Big Challenge variety, then it will impact our identity as leaders. It actually becomes part of us—and usually well before we acquire expertise or even complete competence in facing the challenge. Think back to the people we met in Chapter 1— how might their respective leader identities have shifted as they embraced their Next Big Challenge? I can't speak directly for them, but here are some thoughts:

- For Nancy, the nurse director: Embracing the challenge perhaps means that she sees herself as a conductor, but no longer as a fix-it person. Maybe she will never be completely comfortable in this role, but she will strive to work at it.
- For Sam, the engineer: Embracing the challenge may mean that he now sees himself as a leader, and not just an engineer. He knows that he will make mistakes and feel inadequate from time to time, but he will continue to step up.
- For Angela, the business executive: Embracing the challenge could mean that she realizes that she has a voice, and she will never, ever stop using it. Even if she feels "less than" or like she has nothing to say that others would want to hear, she will persevere.
- And for Mike, university professor and your author: Embracing the challenge means believing that I have something valuable to offer to others, and that owning my own business will enable me to create the impact that I desire. It means being responsible for my own actions and their consequences.

Third, **embracing the challenge means that we seek out help from others.** Perhaps the work we've done so far has been mostly by ourselves, but now we realize that we need to bring others into the picture. We have found and faced the challenge, but now we are realizing that this endeavor is for the long haul, and we need support to continue growing. Asking for help is a sure sign that you are embracing the Next Big Challenge.

10

STRUCTURED SUPPORT FOR THE ME1ST METHOD – AND WHY YOU NEED IT

"If you want to go quickly, go alone. If you want to go far, go together."—AFRICAN PROVERB

L et's take a moment to review what we know so far:

1. You are a leader who is seeking to find, face, and embrace the Next Big Challenge

2. You will face resistance from the system(s), from others, and from yourself

3. Quick fixes generally do not work

4. There's a science of leader development (the **Me1st Method**), but it is going to take some work and has some unique challenges. For example:

- How do you find the Next Big Challenge? How do you refine the picture of what you desire, and how do you sustain the motivation?

- How do you face the Next Big Challenge? Where do you obtain educational resources, both the things you need to know and an accurate picture of how you are doing? How do you create and hone a strategy? What do you do when an experiment doesn't go as planned?
- How do you embrace the Next Big Challenge? Where can you find the support to keep going?

It should be no surprise that seeking help is important. After all, leadership is an inherently *social* phenomenon. It involves relationships among people. And, as we pointed out, one of the main outcomes from the **Me1st Method** is **connectedness**.

So…this is not a solo adventure (or at least it should not be). You need help and support. Certainly, this book is a helpful resource (at least I hope it is if you've made it this far!). But what other kinds of support should you be looking for?

In this chapter, we are going to take a look at various forms of leader development support. Then, I am going to make the case that an all-in-one solution makes the most sense.

TRAINING AND LEARNING

Seeking out knowledge and information is a logical starting point. After all, you are reading this book (or listening to it) as a source of knowledge. In today's world, there is no shortage of information. You can find information by just doing a simple search on the internet about the particular issue that you're facing. You will surely find somebody's blog or article, read it, and get a couple of ideas that help you out. You could also find a paid option, whether it's a simple online course or enrolling in some sort of training through a consulting firm or perhaps even a local university. You could even enroll in some sort of degree program, like getting a master's degree in leadership. There are many good ones available, and a good number are fully online.

It's easy to find information, but much more difficult to find credible and useful information. How do you know if the author or speaker actually knows their stuff? As Abraham Lincoln once said, "Don't believe everything you read on the internet." At least I think that was Abe Lincoln, but it might have been Susan B. Anthony. (Hey! I promised you some dad-joke humor back in the introduction. I'm a man of my word.)

Training comes with an additional challenge: think of a great training program you have attended. Maybe it was a class of some sort, or maybe even a retreat held over multiple days. You went, and you learned a bunch of good information. Maybe it was even interactive, including breakout sessions, projects, and lively Q&A sessions. Finally, you got to the end of that wonderful training and had a great feeling about it.

And then next Monday morning...crickets. You didn't do anything with it. It went on a shelf, and nothing much happened. There was no follow-through, and no changes were made.

That's happened to me many, many times, and I suspect it's happened to you as well. Training—of any sort—has an implementation problem.

ASK YOUR PEERS

A second big option that you have if you're facing a leadership challenge is to ask your friends or peers. Whether this occurs informally in a one-on-one chat, or more formally with a group of people that you trust and meet with regularly, you can benefit from some different insights and perspectives. You can draw on other people's experiences in dealing with a similar problem, and you might receive a little bit of encouragement, and perhaps a little bit of accountability.

Lots of good things can come from talking to peers, but there are some potential downsides, too. How many times have you been in a situation where it devolves into one of two things?

First, it can just become a big bitching session where you're just all complaining about the problem that you're facing. Hey, that certainly feels good in the moment. It's comforting to have that connection around a thought like, "If it wasn't for these idiots, everything would be fine here," but ultimately it doesn't do much good.

The other thing that it can devolve into is a big advice-giving session. Now you might actually be asking for advice. That's fine, that's appropriate. **But I think for most of us, our default is just to start giving advice, even when it's not requested.** It's like we suddenly turn into Vanilla Ice: "If you got a problem, Yo! I'll solve it!" Some of that advice might be helpful. Most of it is not, because it has more to do with the advice-givers need to feel like they're contributing instead of actually helping the person who is seeking support.

COACHING

The third thing that we could do is to seek out some sort of coaching or mentorship. Here, I'm including one-on-one meetings with a more experienced person who can mentor us or help us through situations. But mainly I am focusing on hiring a professional coach to help you through particular challenges. It's a great experience to benefit from somebody who may be has more experience or more knowledge to apply to your particular situation. It's not generalized information; instead, it's very specific to you. There's a sense of a connection in that one-on-one relationship, which can help to embolden you as you go about the difficult business of leading. In an ideal world, you'd be taking this coach around with you on your shoulder, and they would be able to watch everything that you do, every interaction that you have, and be able to give you immediate feedback. In reality, of course, that doesn't happen, but a good coach will help you to draw out what happened, and why. Further, unlike a peer-to-peer relationship, a professional coach is focused on you and you alone; they are not focused on working through their own challenges during your time together.

There are many benefits to coaching, but also some potential traps. Sometimes coaching, like talking to peers, can devolve into just straight-up advice-giving. Now, the coach is no longer acting as a coach, but as more of a consultant. Hey, that person may have some great experience and insight, but if you were hiring that person to solve your problem, I would suggest that you are actually abdicating your role as a leader by outsourcing problem-solving that you need to be doing yourself. Remember, taking a Me1st approach means taking responsibility for the things that you should be doing yourself.

Ultimately, having a *de facto* advice-giving consultant instead of a coach is going to end up hurting you and hurting your team. Unless there is a good give-and-take dynamic with well-defined boundaries between the two people in that relationship, it will eventually undermine itself.

The other challenge here is that no matter how experienced or how engaged that particular coach is, it's still just one person, right? It's still just one set of experiences, one set of knowledge. There are going to be some shortcomings and some gaps in their knowledge. There's never going to be a complete understanding of who you are as a person, because even the best coaches are human, and therefore imperfect and finite.

Why You Need an All-in-One Solution

I would like to suggest that the best approach to leader development is an all-of-the-above approach. In other words, participate in one coherent program so that the strengths of one approach balance out the shortcomings of the other approaches.

I think this is especially true for Next Big Challenge leaders. In my experience, Next Big Challenge leaders desire multiple forms of support, including:

- **Focused 1:1 coaching**

Next Big Challenge leaders know how to support others, but what they often overlook is themselves. They are delightfully surprised that focusing on themselves helps them to notice the unnoticed, create options, and develop their own best thinking. And they want to continue this personal deep dive with confidential, 1:1 coaching support that is both challenging and empathetic.

- **Connection with other leaders**

Next Big Challenge leaders are sometimes faced with challenges that can feel disorienting. They appreciate being able to connect with other leaders who are facing similar challenges.

- **Learning and development that pushes past the superficial**

Next Big Challenge leaders know that generic, off-the-shelf leadership advice may be found in the nearest book, blog, or podcast. They know that much of this advice is like junk food: it tastes good and satisfies temporarily. Next Big Challenge leaders, however, need knowledge that is like whole foods: substantive and providing real nourishment. They also want focused, "micro" learning that is specific and useful.

WHAT DOES THE RESEARCH SAY?

So far, I think we've made a decent, common sense case for why an all-of-the-above approach makes sense. We can also look at it from the perspective of the scientific, peer-reviewed research on leader development. The good news from this research is that, in general, leadership development programs are effective. The other good news is that we know specific ways to make them even more effective. Let me summarize those findings:[1]

First, leadership development programs are usually evaluated along four dimensions:

1. **Satisfaction.** One thing that we know is that a spoonful of sugar really does help the medicine go down. In other words, development tends to be more effective when people feel positive about it. That doesn't mean that it is easy or without pain, but it does mean that the effort expended was worth it.

2. **Learning.** Growing as a leader means that we have learned something. What new knowledge did we gain? What new skills are we able to practice now? What new actions can we take? What new resources do we have? Good leader development results in having something now that we didn't have before.

3. **Application.** Development isn't just about knowing more stuff. It's also about being able to do something new and being a different type of leader—in other words, a leader with a changed or enhanced identity. So we must ask: to what extent can we take our new learning and apply it where it counts? In other words, what can we take out of a classroom, or out of online training, or out of a group meeting, or

out of a one-on-one session with a coach and actually put into practice?

4. **Results.** If I can happily learn new things and apply them, does that mean that I will actually impact anything? Is my team going to get more sales? Is my company going to serve more customers? Am I going to move towards living out my purpose as a leader? Effective leader development programs should be able to answer these questions clearly.

One other thing I'd like to mention from this research. Generally speaking, the **longer the program and the more spaced out the learning is over time, the better our ability to apply it in our real-life situations and the more impactful the results.** Although it's efficient to have an intensive all-day training session, the impact is going to be mitigated vs. spreading the development out.

WHY YOU NEED AN ALL-IN-ONE APPROACH, PART 2

With these things in mind, let's take another look at an all-in-one approach. (And, by the way, these are exactly the reasons why I designed the Me1st Academy the way that I have. There really is a method behind the madness.)

Satisfaction. Honestly, any well-designed learning and development program, group coaching program, or private coaching program should provide satisfaction to the client. Again—not because it is easy, but because it is valuable. However, when we include all of these elements together, we hedge our bets that at least one component will be amazing and the leader will absolutely love it. From a developmental perspective, the high level of satisfaction from one element spills over into the other elements as well. It's called the *halo effect*, and it increases the efficacy of the overall program.

Learning. Again, all three elements should lead to learning. But targeted, self-paced training and learning is squarely focused on this aspect. It's designed to provide us with information about ways of thinking about things, ways of looking at the world, and ways of developing skills.

Application. Good training will usually include insightful exercises, and a good coach will help you to apply what you've learned. However, practicing what you learn is where having groups of peers can really help. Certainly, you can benefit from your peers' experience. But a group of peers also provides a unique opportunity to actually practice. Why? Because as soon as you have a group of peers, you have also formed your own new little social system—and that creates a wonderful opportunity to practice. You can practice deliberately; for example, through role-playing. You can also practice just in the natural functioning of this new little social system that you formed. Group dynamics are going to form, and they're going to form quickly. There are going to be people that talk too much or not enough, there are going to be people that jump in and try to over-perform or under-perform. There are going to be ones that try to bring you into a closeness that might not be helpful, or keep you so far away that that's also not helpful. In short, you can apply what you are learning and practice being a better leader with your peers.

Results. Let me be blunt here: working with an experienced coach is the best "fast-forward pass" to clear results that I know about. Even the best learning and training will only be able to focus on generalities, and group programs—while effective—are slower by nature. A good coach will be listening, and intently asking questions. Then when it's time for the coach to put their expertise into this conversation, it will be short. It will be on point. It will be targeted at whatever it is that's particular to you, rather than generalities. A coach also drives results by giving feedback. A coach is listening intently and thinking about the big picture, what you're doing in the situation that you're describing, how what you're doing is impacting the social system that you are embedded in, and how you might adjust. But a good coach will also provide some immediate feedback. A good coach should be able to say things like, "Hey, wow, you know, I'm listening to this story and I know that you have a lot to say, but to be honest, I'm really having trouble focusing on what it is that you're trying to tell me." A coach will be able to point things out that others might be noticing, but are afraid to say to you.

MYTHS TO BUST

Before we wrap up this chapter, I would like to name—and bust—three common myths about support for leader development.

Myth #1: Coaching and Training is Too Expensive

Let's be frank: quality leadership development is not cheap, especially if you are paying from your own pocket. Year-long one-on-one executive coaching (12 monthly sessions) runs about $5-8K (with much higher fees for C-Level coaching). Similarly, multi-day leader development programs may cost $4K-$6K, and even open-enrollment leader training is often priced in the range of $500—$1500 per seat.

If your organization is of sufficient size to have a dedicated training budget, then these fees should not present a problem. If, however, your organization does not have a budget OR if you are paying out-of-pocket, then you need to do a bit of math.

The key is to maximize value and return-on-investment (ROI). Here are the relevant questions:

1. What financial results would cover the cost of the coaching and training, and even begin to show a return?

2. What is the lifetime value of the coaching and training?

There are many ways to begin to answer these questions, but let me give you a few shortcuts:

1. **For organizational financial ROI, first look to employee retention/turnover.** A good deal of research shows that it costs companies about 1.5—2X annual salary to replace an employee. So do the math. The cost savings resulting from keeping just one employee for just one additional year are significant, and provide an ROI on coaching training of 5X, 10X, or even 40-50X. It is incredibly cost-effective.

2. **For individual financial ROI, first look to the value of a promotion or a new job** (which, as a Next Big Challenge leader, is often a strong possibility). Figure a 10% raise based on your current salary (which is a reasonable and probably conservative number). That raise alone almost certainly covered your coaching and training. Now factor in that raise for every year remaining in your career. Once again, incredibly cost-effective.

Both of these examples are simple, reliable, straightforward financial calculations. There are also other indirect benefits (e.g., raising employee engagement, which results in ROI) and qualitative benefits (e.g., self-growth as a person that spills over into other areas of life, like family).

Bottom line: if you yourself experience sticker-shock, or you meet with resistance from your boss or HR department, take a deep breath and do some quick math. You will see the value, and so will others.

Myth #2: I Don't Have Time or Headspace for This Right Now

Common refrains for this myth include:

"Training takes too long"

"I don't have time in my schedule"

"I'm so focused on other things that I don't have the bandwidth for it right now"

I respect these objections, but once again let me be frank: If you are a Next Big Challenge leader, you need support right now.

Yes, you're busy and maybe feeling overwhelmed. This is also precisely the point at which support will be most valuable and learning and growth the most efficient.

The key here is to focus on *flexible* training and support. One drawback to a coaching-only approach is that it's not very efficient to pay somebody to teach you one (very expensive) hour at a time, right? You're paying really high rates to just absorb information.

Instead, find something that offers on-demand learning on the topics you need right now. Find something that offers multiple contact points: focused, intense 1:1 coaching, but also interaction with other leaders. Find something that offers long-term access because development is a back-and-forth process (not a one-and-done event).

Myth #3: Coaching and Training Don't Work

Once again, I respect the objection. But let me suggest that it is actually *poorly designed and executed* coaching and training that do not work.

We mentioned these things in Chapter 4, but they bear repeating here. The reasons why leader development programs don't work are:

1. Coaching devolves into advice-giving consulting

2. Training is focused almost exclusively on skill development, and doesn't address deeper issues

3. The role of the leader is presented as mainly motivating others, rather than focusing on self

Actually, I have an even better way to bust this last myth. I'm going to show you that leader development can work if done right. Let's work together and get you some tangible results, beginning in the next chapter.

Part III:

Time to Take the First Steps

11

CREATING YOUR PERSONAL LEADERSHIP PURPOSE STATEMENT

"If you don't know where you're going, any road will get you there"

"Would you tell me, please, which way I ought to go from here?"
"That depends a good deal on where you want to get to," said the Cat.
"I don't much care where–" said Alice.
"Then it doesn't matter which way you go," said the Cat.
"–so long as I get SOMEWHERE," Alice added as an explanation.
"Oh, you're sure to do that," said the Cat, "if you only walk long enough."
–LEWIS CARROLL, *Alice's Adventures in Wonderland*

This is the actual quote from *Alice in Wonderland*. I love that it focuses on the journey, the road. It is a reminder that we are always and inescapably on a journey. Time marches onward. Life is lived forward. There's no opting out of the journey, for even if we do our best to stay in place, life will continue to move along without us.

We are all in motion, all headed somewhere.

But where, exactly? And, how do we get there? And, what do we do along the way?

Simple enough questions, right?

In this chapter, I am going to help you find your purpose as a leader as you create your Personal Leadership Purpose Statement (PLPS)—a concise and living two-page document that serves as our leadership constitution. As a reminder, the PLPS serves several purposes:

- First and foremost, it provides tremendous guidance towards finding our Next Big Challenge
- During the most challenging times (a.k.a. our anxiety shit storms), it reminds us of our ultimate aspirations
- When opportunities arise, it guides us to make good decisions
- When actual danger appears, it protects us by giving us tools to overcome the danger

A PLPS consists of three parts: vision, mission, and values.[1] Let's create those one at a time.

CONSTRUCTING A PERSONAL LEADERSHIP PURPOSE STATEMENT

1. Vision of Ideal Life

The first part is a vivid picture of your ideal life at some point in the future. How far into the future? There's no magical timeframe, but in my experience about 5 years is an optimal horizon. That's long enough to bring about change, but near enough that there is some reasonable trajectory from now until then. Whatever the timeframe, we are aiming for about 2 paragraphs that describe our desired future state. Think of this part as a great painting—a true work of art.

In constructing this vision, keep three things in mind:

- The picture we create needs to be vivid, with real, concrete examples (showing, not telling)
- It should focus on both professional and personal aspects of life
- It should be big, bold, and unedited

Concrete examples

Let's do some imagining together. Think about the last business presentation you sat through. Charts, stats, PowerPoint slides...endless slides. Now re-imagine Dr. Martin Luther King's "I Have a Dream Speech" as a similar type of business presentation. Imagine him showing a slide with a bullet-pointed list of actions to make a more just America.

Go on, imagine it.

Important? Yes. Energizing and compelling? No way.

Now imagine the clips you have seen of that speech. Hear him saying, "We will not be satisfied until justice rolls down like waters and righteousness like a mighty stream." Imagine that mighty stream. Imagine standing on the crowded National Mall in August. Imagine how real, how welcome a mighty stream would have felt that day, and imagine how it would have felt to desire righteousness in the same way.

Important? Vitally. Energizing and compelling? Absolutely.

That is the same type of vivid imagery to aim for in your ideal life vision. Use words to represent images that are important to you and will spur you to action. It might not be as grandiose as MLK's words (then again, it might!), but it should be meaningful for you.

Here's one from my own PLPS: "I enjoy rejuvenating alone time in my library with its floor-to-ceiling bookshelves and on long walks." While other parts of my vision involve my family and friends, this line is just for me. A room full of old books, a big-ass recliner, a fireplace, and a view of something beautiful—what more could a fella want? Well, I'll tell you what: multiple walking routes involving both nature and civilization right out the front door. That's the perfect blend of activities for an introspective professor like me.

PROFESSIONAL AND PERSONAL

This is our vision of the ideal life, and it should include all important aspects, both professional and personal. Imagine living out your deep sense of purpose and calling—or perhaps imagine the process of discovering what that purpose is as you travel the world and meet new people. Imagine the people you will help and how the world—or at least one little part of it—will be better because of your efforts.

Here is part of my PLPS that is professionally-focused: "I am creating over $20M of total identifiable value to my clients each year." Yes, that's right. I want to be able to see the value I bring. Of course, not all value is easily translated into dollars and cents. Yet, at a minimum, I want to see people flourish with my help, and putting a tangible goal on it makes it that much easier to gauge.

Now, tie your professional and personal lives together. For example, I wrote, "Megan (my wife) and I spend a good deal of time discerning how to use our substantial resources to make a lasting impact—and we laugh a lot." I desire to do well financially, but the 'doing well' has a purpose behind it. The financial outlays are all part of the vision.

BIG, BOLD, UNEDITED

Now is not the time for thinking small thoughts, or editing ourselves because we think our dreams are out of reach. Don't worry—there will be a time and a place to appropriately temper our expectations, but that time and place is not here.

Perhaps your vision includes living in a particular type of home or location, or having the ability to travel whenever and wherever you like. Perhaps it is seeing your organization thrive in its mission. For me, it's about being fully engaged in every area of life: in teaching, coaching, research, family, and friends.

Whatever your desire is, try expanding it, try to go crazy with it, try to be outrageous. See where it takes you. Remember, the purpose of the vision is to remind us of our ultimate aspirations during both good and bad times.

Give it some thought, and draft a vision. Again, about two paragraphs —perhaps one is focused on the professional, and the other on the personal.

Helpful Hint: You aren't going to nail it perfectly the first time around. Draft it, and let it sit a day or two. Come back to it. What do you like? What needs to be tweaked?

2. Mission in Life

A well-crafted mission statement forms the second part of our PLPS. A mission statement brings shape and direction to our actions to help us realize the vision. It serves as the primary roadmap for our leader's journey.

As we mentioned earlier in the book, a clearly defined mission helps us to do several things:

- It gives us direction to say *yes* to the very best opportunities
- It helps us to *resist the temptation* to say yes to potentially bad or harmful choices
- Perhaps most importantly, it gives us permission to say *no* to what might be very good opportunities, but ones that are not suited to us

Let me give you an example. I make my home in Rochester, NY, which is also the headquarters of Wegmans Food Markets. Wegmans is annually named as one of the best places to work in America, and shopping there is an experience in itself. Wegmans' mission is "helping people live healthier, better lives through food." Several years ago, Jack DePeters, then the Senior Vice President of Store Operations, was asked in an interview how much autonomy Wegmans gives store managers to make decisions. His answer was that they have plenty of autonomy, as long as their decisions are in alignment with the mission and values of the company. He said something to the effect of "we don't want them selling used cars in the parking lot." [2]

Think about his answer for a second. Selling used cars is a noble and necessary business. With Wegmans' reputation and operational know-how, they'd probably be pretty good (and profitable) at it. But it would ultimately be a distraction that would prevent them from being the best food retailers that they can be.

In the same way, our mission can put healthy limits on what we will and will not do. My mission in life includes this line:

I strive to notice the unnoticed, create options, and develop my own best thinking and actions—and help others to do the same.

If I cannot see a clear path to accomplish one or more of those outcomes, then I will not spend more than a nominal amount of time or energy on it.

Remember, a well-defined mission in life helps to tell us what to do when we need to make important life decisions. Like your vision, you probably won't get this part just right at first either. That's OK—draft it and try it on for size. To use our earlier language, create a provisional identity, and then see if that identity should stay or be discarded.

3. Values Identified and Defined

While a mission is excellent to refer to when we are faced with important decisions, clearly-defined values serve as a day-in, day-out guide for helping us to live well.

In her excellent book *Dare to Lead*, Brené Brown points out two important dynamics about values.[3] First, in order to be useful, they need to be very limited. Echoing Jim Collins's admonition of "if you have more than three priorities, you have no priorities," she suggests that we have a maximum of two foundational values. Second, in order to be useful, the values need to be put into action in real and tangible ways. For example, she writes, "One of my courage behaviors is 'Don't choose silence over what is right. It's not my job to make others more comfortable or to be liked by everyone.'"

Following her admonitions, we want to name and define two—and only two—values. We also want to provide clear examples of when we are and are not living out those values. For example, *wisdom*—which I define as the pursuit of being excellent at knowing, being, feeling, and doing—is one of my core values. I am living out the value of wisdom when I deliberately put myself into new situations in order to learn, grow, and practice. Towards this end, over the past few years, I have taken a drawing class at a local art museum and learned to play hockey (sort of) in an adult developmental league.

For each of the two values, provide three clear examples of situations in which you are living out that value well. Also, provide three examples of when you are NOT living it—when you are missing the mark.

Speaking of wisdom, here are two words of wisdom to consider. First, we have provided a list of values as part of your bonuses with this book. Look at a few to begin the process—it's a helpful shortcut. Second, don't be surprised if this is harder than it first seems—harder, in fact, than creating your vision or mission. It literally took me two weeks of consideration to narrow my list to two: wisdom and freedom. Once I had a shortlist of 4-5 possible candidates, I would "try them on" for a day or two by linking my actions to one or more of the possible values.

Knowing and living our core values are incredibly useful tools for navigating the dangerous road of leadership.

CONCLUDING THOUGHTS

We now have the knowledge we need to create a clear and compelling PLPS that will help us to find the Next Big Challenge. But one question remains: is the PLPS set in stone, never to be changed?

Of course, it isn't. Leadership—like life itself—is an iterative process. Things that were important yesterday may be almost meaningless tomorrow, and vice versa. So how will we know when it is time to change our purpose? The answer will depend on each individual person of course.

Think of your PLPS as the written document that best represents your ideal self; that is, the person and leader you wish to become. As you put on your "ideal-self" identity and act accordingly, pay attention to internal and external cues that the PLPS does indeed reflect your ideal self. Do you feel energized and enthused? Do frustrations somehow seem pleasant at some level? Are others responding to your ideal self as you expected? Are you producing positive results? If the answers are generally yes, then keep going. If you find that the answers are increasingly no, then it may be time to revisit your PLPS.

Leadership is hard work, but when we have a clearly defined sense of purpose, we are more ready to do the hard work. With the Cheshire Cat's words to Alice in mind, let's endeavor to live and lead with purpose.

12

CREATING A TEAM CHARTER

"The speed of the boss is the speed of the team."—LEE IACOCCA

I f you took the information about teams in Chapter 7 (Motivate) to heart, then you probably have a good sense of what you would like to see from your team. If you do not, consider revisiting that information before continuing. Our purpose in this chapter is to move from our own thinking into strategic action with our team by creating a team charter.

WHAT IS A TEAM CHARTER?

A team charter is a team-generated constitution—a foundational document that governs how the team functions. While there is no one-size-fits-all team charter, the process that I am going to outline and the format I am going to suggest should provide a solid foundation for most teams in most situations. Of course, feel free to adapt as needed.

Step 1: A Good, Old-Fashioned Complaint Session (aka Whining and Moaning)

This is one of my all-time favorite activities when I'm teaching. Whether I'm teaching undergraduates, graduate students, or executives, everybody loves this exercise—because everyone can relate to it.

Here's how it works:

1. Get a stack of scrap paper, Post-it Notes, or 3 x 5 cards—basically you just need many little blank pieces of paper. Give each team member a goodly supply.

2. Instruct everyone to begin writing down things they hate about working in teams—one item per piece of paper. Have them immediately place the papers into a box or bowl in the middle of the table.

- Something that you've experienced in the past
- Something that you fear might happen in the future
- Something that is annoying currently

Note: Some people might claim that they love working in teams and have never had a bad experience. They're lying.

3. Go through the responses one by one and compile a master list (e.g., on a whiteboard or flip chart).

Note: Be prepared for a lot of head-nodding and even some laughs.

4. Sort the master list into two broad categories:

- Responses that have to do with the work itself
- Responses that have to do with people

Congratulations! You now have a self-generated, usable list of *felt* issues or problems that you can use to create a better team charter. Specifically, you now have a checklist that will help you determine whether your team charter is adequate to address the major concerns of the team.

Before we begin to construct the charter, I do want to offer a word of wisdom here. In academia, we have a running joke that, over time, a class syllabus becomes a historical record of everything that has gone wrong in prior classes.

- Students missing deadlines? Amend syllabus to include penalties
- Student turning in a paper with no citations? Specify that papers must include citations
- Students claiming that the internet crashed right before the deadline? State that last-minute internet outages should be expected, and will therefore not be a valid excuse

The same thing can happen with this fun exercise. While we are being playful by soliciting complaints, and while it really does produce a list of things to pay attention to, don't let it become the main focus. And certainly, don't let the team charter become like a 10-year old syllabus, addressing every issue that every person ever had.

Step 2: Writing the Team Charter

I suggest that the charter should have two main parts:

- Mission (what we do—the work)
- Vision & Values (how we do things and the results)

This is where your own best thinking from back in Chapter 6 can help. You have already thought through these issues yourself, and are able to provide that input in an appropriate way. This is where you need to make some decisions:

- To what extent is this going to be a team-driven process, really?
- Do I have non-negotiables that must be there (and what are they)?
- For parts that are negotiable, when and how will I give my own input (if at all)?

By the way, this is a great topic to discuss with a coach or with peers prior to engaging with your team. This is truly one of the topics in which a conversation or two with others who have no direct stake in the team can be very helpful.

Once you have a plan for how you intend to show up, it's time to begin.

1. Mission

A) What is the work?

As we mentioned back in Chapter 6, for many teams, the mission (the work) is often already defined, at least partially. In this section, we want to state that mission clearly and succinctly. We also want to make sure that everyone agrees that this is indeed the mission.

B) Getting the work done: authority, accountability, and oversight

In this section, we want to specify the process—*not for doing the work itself* (which should be outlined in other, more flexible formats, like having Standard Operating Procedures)—but rather for *making sure the work gets done*. For doing this, I suggest making sure the process for assigning authority, accountability, and oversight is clear. **This may be the single most important part of the team charter.**

First of all, we need to ensure that someone has the **authority** to carry out that task. Someone has to have decision-making power. Someone needs to be authorized to use organizational resources (time, money, people) to achieve the goals. I want to emphasize this point: is absolutely critical to decide which individuals will be empowered to complete the task(s). This is how we include the element of *freedom* into our teams.

Second of all, that person needs to be held **accountable** for completing those tasks. This can be achieved through traditional project management methodologies, but it could also be as simple as identifying the task, what the completed task will look like, and the deadline. We don't have to get into specifying how they do it or how they work on it, but simply focusing on what it looks like when it is accomplished. We have that level of accountability and a way to track that.

The third element is that another person needs to have **oversight** over the person who has the authority and accountability. Perhaps it's you as the team lead, perhaps it's someone else on the team, or perhaps it's someone external, but somebody needs to be making sure that things are getting done. There needs to be that "+1", that second layer of oversight to make sure that things are happening.

By the way, notice how having accountability and oversight are practical applications of *wisdom* in teams. If we have a clear shared understanding of these three things—authority, accountability, and oversight—then we will be set up for success in completing tasks.

Checkpoint: Make sure that the process you come up with addresses any items related to authority, accountability, or oversight from your Complaint List

2. Vision & Values

A) What does it look like when this team is flourishing?

Here, we want to create a vivid picture of what life is like when this team is flourishing—the work is excellent, the people are happy, and all is well. This is where your own thinking may be especially helpful. As the leader, can you paint or at least sketch a vision of a better future? Can you then invite the team to co-create that picture with you?

Here are a few things to keep in mind for this part:

- Use bold, action-oriented descriptions (if people were watching a video about the day in the life of the flourishing team, they should be able to see visible signs of that flourishing)
- Use the Complaint List as a starting point—if it is on the list, then consider what the opposite would be

B) Supporting the team: communication, tough conversations, and cohesion

In order for people to feel connected to the team, to one another, and to the vision for the team, there are a few things that we need to have in place. First of all, we need to make sure that we have defined how the people on the team are going to operate with one another. What are the norms? How do we do things on this team? To answer these questions, there are three non-negotiables that all teams must specify.

First, as a tactical move, we need to be explicit about our **communication channels and how we use them**. When we work as a team, are we talking face-to-face? Are we talking virtually? Are we using email? Can we text each other? Should we be using a team-focused app like Slack or Microsoft Teams? In what instances do we use those different forms of communication?

For example, we can specify that Slack is appropriate for routine tasks. However, if it is something that requires more creativity and in-depth discussion, then perhaps we have a face-to-face or virtual meeting to kick off the process. Then we'll follow it up with a thread in Slack, where we're bouncing ideas back and forth. We'll also specify how we are going to make our final decision. Perhaps we agree to discuss until we reach a consensus, or we agree that after a specified amount of time, one person (or a small group of people) is responsible for making that decision.

The second thing we need is a framework for having **tough conversations.** One of the biggest dynamics that undermine teams is that people either avoid issues or deal with them through force. It's nothing malicious usually, but in effect, somebody will just get up and just start talking, or be so set on a particular position that it has the net effect of bludgeoning other people into submission.

Instead of avoiding or forcing, we need to develop a framework for people on the team to be able to have tough conversations. One of the most effective ways to do that is to develop a framework and some common language that signifies, "This is going to be a tough conversation." Years ago, I was attending some leadership training. I don't remember much of that particular training, but one thing I do remember was that the group had their own vocabulary. The key phrase here was, "I need to meet you at the line." That was their internal signal that they need to step up to this imaginary line, and they would talk about the issues. Sure, those conversations were still difficult and awkward, but simply giving the signal that it was going to be a tough conversation went a long way towards helping to resolve issues.

The third thing we need to figure out is a way to encourage **team cohesion**. Think about the best teams that you've ever been a part of. There is that sense of camaraderie—love, even—where everyone is on the same page and you've got each other's back. That's team cohesion. It's that glue that holds teams together and allows teams to perform and achieve uncommon results.

How does that happen? How can we best utilize our face-to-face time to get people to bond, and how can we replicate that in a virtual environment? Depending on your team and your setup, there are a million different ways to establish cohesion, but the point is that needs to be included. Maybe it's scheduling time for people to go do their own work undisturbed, scheduling time for collaboration, and scheduling time to socialize. The key idea here is that team cohesion does not usually occur without some intentional actions.

C) Other Values

To this point, I have specified items that I believe every team charter ought to contain. If you are with me in that line of thinking, then here is the part where you can really put your team's own uniqueness into play. This process is very similar to the one we used to create the values section of your PLPS, but with a few caveats:

- We are aiming for *three* core team values (not two)
- We want them to reflect the team's collective thinking

Remember, these values should be useful for guiding team actions, especially when unexpected challenges arise. Here's what I suggest you do:

1. Use a list of common values (you can use the one that comes with this book)

2. Have each team member specify their top 3 team values

3. Compile the results and focus on the top 3-5 (use 5, unless there is a sharp drop-off in voting after #3 or #4 on the list)

4. Come up with a preliminary definition for each of the values, as well as descriptions of three ways each in which the team is/is not living out that value

5. With the complete list of 5 defined and described values, see if there is a way to refine or combine

6. Narrow the list to three and only three core values

7. If needed, make any final tweaks to the definition and the is/is not descriptions for each

Congratulations! You now have a complete draft of a team charter. Before finalizing it, though, there are just a few more things to do:

Checkpoint: Make sure that the charter addresses all of the major complaints from the Complaint List (or, if it does not, be clear on why)

Add one last piece: Specify when the charter will be revisited and possibly amended. For example, will it be based on time? Quarterly? Or perhaps when there is turnover on the team or a specific goal is achieved?

Now, for real, congratulations! You have your team charter!

Concluding Thoughts

Before we move on, let's pause a moment to consider what a Me1st approach looks like for teams. One of my coaches shared this prompt with me, "Ask yourself two questions: what am I responsible for and who am I responsible to?" Now, isn't that a great pair of questions to ask? If we apply them in the framework we just covered, we now have a series of actionable questions that will help us to define ourselves in the context of our team functioning:

1. Which task(s) am I responsible for?
2. Which people do I oversee, and for which of their tasks?
3. Who am I responsible for communicating with?
4. To what extent am I responsible for team cohesion?
5. How will I live out the team values?

These are good questions, certainly. But I think the real power is when we add the word NOT to them:

1. Which task(s) am I NOT responsible for?
2. Which people do I NOT oversee, and for which of their tasks?
3. Who am I NOT responsible for communicating with?
4. To what extent am I NOT responsible for team cohesion?
5. How am I NOT living out the team values?

Now you might be asking, "Hey Mike, doesn't this kind of thinking create an environment of 'not my problem' and 'not my job'?"

Well, my answer would be, "Yes. Absolutely. That's kind of the point."

You see, taking a Me1st approach does not mean we will not or should not jump in to do whatever is needed on occasion, or that we refuse to speak up or call out problems. What it does mean is that when we do more, we do so thoughtfully, with the full awareness that **there is a trade-off happening** and there very well may be **an underlying systemic issue that needs to be addressed.** In other words, the mantra of "be a team player" without clearly defined roles and boundaries is just manipulation. Showing up as well-defined, emotionally mature individuals opens the lock to better performance and true connectedness.

Just to wrap up here: as we are working to discover what our ideal team looks like, we need to focus on two key characteristics: getting the work done and supporting the team. If we can keep those two things in mind, we'll be well on our way to creating a high-performing team that achieves clear results.

13

CREATING AN ORGANIZATIONAL CHANGE MANIFESTO

"People don't fear change; they fear loss"—RON HEIFETZ
AND MARTY LINSKY

In this chapter, I'd like to continue the conversation we began all the way back in Chapter 6 concerning bottom-line organizational results. If you recall, we focused on creating your own personal vision of what life could be like—for you, for your team, and for your organization—if you were killing it on your KPIs and really living out the organization's vision, mission, and values. If you followed the prompts there, you have a great start—a clear sense of the motivation for acting.

Awesome. But what do we do with it?

That's our focus in this chapter. Our goal is to add in the education, strategy, and testing, and to create a plan for lasting change focused on organizational results. I prefer to call it the **organizational change manifesto**. (I know, I know. The term *manifesto* conjures up a picture of an eccentric recluse banging away on an old typewriter. But I like the term anyway. It literally means "able to be seen" and that is what we are doing: making a visible plan for change).

Allow me to acknowledge that there are books and training courses and gurus and podcasts and articles that all talk about organizational change. This is a huge topic and everyone has an opinion or a philosophy on how to go about doing it. It's not possible to go even 10% into everything that could be said about this topic, so what I want to do here is to lay out some basic frameworks of what I have found to be the most important things to keep in mind as we initiate the change initiative in the organization.

EDUCATION: UNDERSTANDING ROLES IN CHANGE

The first thing to understand about creating change is the different roles that are involved with it. A role is simply an expected pattern of behavior. Think about a role in a movie: it's a person playing a part. If you're playing the villain, we, the viewers, expect to see a certain set of behaviors we associate with 'villain'; otherwise, if you're acting like a completely good person, you're not really the villain.

Coaches Daryl Conner and Mary Beth O'Neill offer a framework that I think is very helpful in this regard.[1] They outline four distinct roles that must be in place in order for change to move forward. Moreover, they emphasize that there must **be clarity around who is playing what role**. Here are the roles:

- **Sponsors**: The person or persons that have the authority and the resources to create change. In an organization, this will usually be somebody that's more senior, often at the C-level, and maybe even the CEO. This is the person who can say, "Yes, I put my stamp of approval on this initiative. This is the direction we want to go on it. This is what we're going to do."

(**Note**: We often also have sub-sponsors: people that are also providing authority and resources, but for a smaller area of responsibility).

- **Implementers**: The people that are actually doing the change; the ones who are carrying out the change and learning to do things differently. For example, if we're doing a change initiative around a new enterprise system, implementors are the people that are actually putting that new system in place and supporting it. This role especially includes those people who will be using the new system.

- **Advocates**: The people that see the need for a change and generate ideas to facilitate it. Advocates may even make some suggestions or come up with a plan to drive change, but they don't have the full authority or resources to do it on their own. So, an effective advocate needs to be somebody who can get support from a sponsor. (**Note**: by virtue of having thought through your vision in Chapter 6, you are already beginning to act in the advocate role.)

- **Change Agents**: The people that help to facilitate the change. These are the people that are adding expertise and adding resources to help this change initiative work. Change agents can be people who are internal or external to the organization, so consultants and coaches may act in this role. Change agents may also be third parties who are providing needed resources (e.g., a new software system) to help the change initiative go through.

It is important to note that while these are four clearly defined roles, it's possible for one person to hold different roles simultaneously. For instance, an advocate can also act as a sponsor if the advocate has the appropriate authority and resources to be able to do that.

Also, note that one of the biggest traps here is when we're not clear on what roles a particular person is fulfilling. This trap often shows up with respect to internal or external consultants. A consultant's role is to act as a change agent: facilitating change, coaching, teaching, and perhaps even providing some resources. **Ultimately, however, a consultant is not responsible for enacting change.** I personally refuse to take on one of those other roles. When it comes to change initiatives, I am a change agent. I'm there to help facilitate the change. I'm not there to create the change. That is not what I do. And more importantly, it's not a responsible act on my part as an outside consultant. I'm going to leave eventually, and this project is going to wrap up—for better or for worse. If I jump in and do things myself, I'm taking away responsibility that belongs to someone else. Further, I have impaired their ability to facilitate that lasting change.

EDUCATION: BARRIERS AND ENABLERS OF CHANGE

The other dynamic that we need to think about concerns common barriers to change and ways to overcome them. Barriers are simply common obstacles that slow down, stop, or in some cases even reverse change. Enablers to change are tactics and techniques we can use to overcome the barriers.

INDIVIDUAL BARRIERS TO CHANGE

First, we want to understand barriers at the individual level—those things that might stand in the way of a change initiative that belong to an individual person. Often these barriers particularly impact those in the implementer role, but they can impact the others as well. The first one is kind of a two-parter: **a need for security, which is often coupled with fear.** Anytime there's a change—even if there's a real chance that this might make things better off—the change is still upsetting the status quo. It's upsetting the equilibrium of the overall system, and that creates challenges. So even if the system isn't great, even if it's not completely healthy, our natural human tendency is to just stay put, because the current system, no matter how bad it is, provides a certain level of security.

Along with that felt sense of security, change is often associated with fear. But fear of what? This is where things get really interesting. The quote at the beginning of this chapter is from a wonderful book called *Leadership on the Line* by Ron Heifetz and Marty Linsky from Harvard University.[2] They write, "People don't fear change; they fear loss." It's not that people are afraid of having a new way of doing things or new equipment to use; instead, it's a fear of losing what they have currently.

Another individual barrier to change is a close cousin of these two: **habits.** You've undoubtedly heard it said, and it's true: humans are creatures of habit. We get comfortable doing the same things over and over, even if they're not as effective or efficient as they could be. We develop habits because the human brain is basically lazy. If we can take a shortcut to avoid expending brain energy, we will usually do it.

On a related note, our final individual barrier to change is **selective perception**, which is simply limiting what we pay attention to in order to reinforce our current focus or belief system. Our minds are wired in such a way that we are constantly scanning the environment for evidence that supports what we already believe to be true. We're always looking for evidence that confirms our own opinion. Put more simply, if you're looking for something that tells you that you're right, you're going to find it.

ORGANIZATIONAL BARRIERS TO CHANGE

The first barrier at the organization level is simply the **history of the organization** itself. If the organization has had limited change in the past, or at least in the recent past, that's going to be a barrier. Successful change involves a good deal of effort and skill. If we haven't had a chance to develop those recently as an organization, it's going to be hard to implement them.

The second potential barrier involves the **structure of the organization**. Structure refers to recognizing all of the tasks that need to be accomplished, how those tasks are divided, and how they are eventually grouped back together and assigned to different people. For example, if we're trying to create new products through our R & D department and then sell them through the Sales department, but the R & D department and the Sales department are not talking to each other, then R & D may be coming up with something that people don't want, and Sales may be trying to sell something that R & D can't produce.

Number three may be the biggest organizational barrier of all: **the culture of the organization**. Culture is simply 'the way we do things around here'. More specifically, it's the set of assumptions that we have, the values that we hold, and the actions that we take on a regular basis. One of my favorite phrases to describe culture is 'those things which are accepted and familiar'. I'll give you a somewhat mundane example. As I mentioned before, for several years I worked as a buyer in a major department store chain. The store—like every organization—had its quirks that become part of the culture. This particular one was during the early internet days, so we still shared a lot of information on good, old-fashioned, printed-out paper. The quirk for this organization was that anything that we printed out had to be printed in landscape format (as opposed to portrait format).

Everything. And it was funny because you could tell when somebody was brand new to the organization by how they printed. More importantly, the sender lost credibility simply because the report was printed in the 'wrong' direction. This one little quirk was a manifestation of an intense focus on minutiae that stopped many efforts at change dead in their tracks.

We can break down the parts of an organizational culture even further. Let's look at three different aspects, beginning with **norms**. Norms refer to the standard way that we do things, especially regarding what we think of as right/wrong, or at least better/worse. From my department store experience: the workday unofficially began between 8 and 9, with junior people arriving before senior people. And 5:30 was the accepted quitting time. One day, my boss got pulled into a meeting at about 4:30. When he still hadn't returned at 5:30, I decided to leave for the day. Boy! Did I get an earful the next morning about "never leaving if I am in a meeting because I might need something." It was as if I was a moral failure for leaving work "on time." Keep in mind, my boss was a decent guy with a big heart, but in those situations, he was a stickler for the rules. Can you envision the struggle that would follow if someone decided to try to change that particular norm?

Another aspect of culture is **relationship dynamics.** I seem to be on a roll, so I'll use another department store example. I actually worked in two different divisions within the same corporation. In the one division, buyers (like my boss) and assistant buyers (like me) did not eat lunch together unless it was a business lunch with a vendor. It was not part of the culture to eat at your desk, so around 12:30, several of the buyers would go to one food court or out to a park. The assistant buyers would go to a different food court or park—and never the two shall meet. This practice reinforced a very hierarchical structure within that division. In contrast, in the other division where I worked, it was perfectly normal and acceptable for everybody to go to lunch together: buyers, assistant buyers, vice presidents, administrative staff—really just whoever happened to be around. Whoever wanted to go to lunch at 12:30, just went. This practice helped to reinforce a genuine open-door policy in that division. It wasn't that hierarchy didn't exist (it did), but rather everyone was focused on the same goal, and who ate lunch together wasn't at the forefront.

The third and perhaps most important aspect of culture concerns **power dynamics**. Power is simply the ability to get someone else to do something, right? In a particular organizational culture, it is important to understand who has the power. Even more importantly, if we are contemplating a change, we need to understand how the power dynamics will shift. Who will be losing power? Who will be gaining power?

ENABLERS OF CHANGE

With so many different barriers to effective change (both individual and organizational), it is understandable that any change initiative may be daunting. So how can we overcome these barriers? How can we enable change? Let's look at a few ways:

First, we can provide reliable **education and communication**, including both focused training and general awareness. For example, if we're implementing a new enterprise system, certainly hands-on training about how to use that is needed to adapt to the new system. But education can also just be sort of more philosophical education of, "Hey, this is a thing. This is coming. We need to be ready." Just yesterday I had a guest speaker who works for a bank and is tasked with developing underserved markets—in particular the Hispanic and Latino markets. One of the things that she showed us was demographic information put out by the U.S. Census Bureau that shows that by 2045, there will not be a majority ethnic group in the United States. In other words, white people will be under 50%. Whites will still be the single largest group, but it will be under 50% and that number will keep dropping. Her punchline to this fact is, "If we want to stay viable, we need to figure out how to serve the Hispanic and Latino markets well—not just to squeeze every dollar out of them."

Another way is to bring about support is through **negotiation**. Negotiation is a pretty big topic, so let's focus on what I think is the most important ingredient to successful negotiations: **focusing on underlying interests rather than surface-level positions**. In other words, understand what people really desire rather than on whatever position they happen to present. Here's a classic story from negotiations training:

Two guys walk into a store, and they intend on getting oranges. They arrive at the same time and see that there is only one box of oranges for sale. They both start grabbing the box and end up having a little scuffle that ends up with the oranges flying into a nearby trash can. The whole box is now completely unusable. And the one guy says to the other one, "I was really looking forward to making some fresh-squeezed orange juice with these oranges, and I really needed the whole box." The second guy looks back at him with a perplexed look and says, "Wow, well, I was planning on using the rinds to make some orange chutney."

One person wanted to make juice. One person wanted to make chutney. Had they talked about it, they could have figured out what their underlying interests were. They could have arrived at a negotiated settlement that would have completely benefited both parties. Instead, they ended up with nothing. This is the essence of negotiating based on interests (making juice or chutney), not positions (I want the oranges!). It can be a very powerful tool for overcoming resistance to change.

To wrap this up, I'm briefly going to mention a few more tactics that can be useful. The first is figuring out a way to get more **people participating,** and in doing so, obtaining their support. This is the classic "get buy-in" approach. If we can get people to have a voice, or better yet, to participate in this overall change initiative, those people are more likely to support it because now they have a sense of ownership, a sense of efficacy. Second, **look for allies**. Allies are others in the organization who share similar interests and want to see similar outcomes. There is power in numbers. A word of warning, though: remember that allies are different from friends or confidants. You need not (and often *should* not) share undue affection or information with allies.

The final two tactics should be used carefully, thoughtfully, and sparingly. Unintended consequences abound, but you should be aware of them. First, you can resort to **manipulation**. You have the option of dangling rewards or punishments for getting compliance with needed change. As I'm writing this in late 2021, we are in the middle of the COVID-19 pandemic. We're at the stage where some companies are requiring all employees to be vaccinated, or they will lose their jobs. That's manipulation—perhaps necessary or justified, but manipulation nonetheless. Finally, sometimes it's worth considering **replacing people** who are resistant to change with other people who are more open to it. Sometimes this tactic is necessary but should be used as a last resort after other attempts have failed.

STRATEGY: WRITING THE CHANGE MANIFESTO

We now have our motivators from Chapter 6, as well as a solid education about the factors that help (and hurt) a successful change initiative. Now it's time to create your manifesto—your written strategy and plan for action.

1. Create a One Page Summary

Create a one-page summary of your overall plan by creating a matrix. Along the top, create a column for each person or group you need to play a role in the change, beginning with yourself. To prompt your thinking, consider all stakeholders (a stakeholder is any person who group who either helps to drive the change or is impacted by the change, or both).

Along the side, from top to bottom, create a row for each of the change elements we just mentioned:

Roles

- Sponsor
- Implementer
- Advocate
- Change Agent

Individual Barriers to Change

- Need for security/fear
- Habits
- Selective perception

Organizational Barriers to Change

- History of organization
- Structure of organization
- Culture of organization
- Norms

- Relationship dynamics
- Power dynamics

Enablers of Change

- Education and communication
- Negotiation
- Participation
- Potential ally
- Manipulation
- Replace

With your matrix set up, begin to fill in the cells. Make a short note (a comment or a question) about how the item in the row (role, barrier, enabler) might be relevant to each person or group. Some might be very clear (e.g., my boss needs to be a sponsor), while others might be a question that needs more information (e.g., Larry in accounting seems to have a high need for security, so how will I confirm this observation and address it?). Still others might be not applicable at all (e.g., Mike is a tenured professor, so I can't replace him even if I'd like to).

The overarching goal is to have a summary of all the possible things you might need to address in the course of the change. If you've done a thorough job, it is likely to look pretty intimidating! That's OK...we have a plan to cut it down to size.

2. Analyze the One Page Summary

Let's take a look at that matrix and begin to sort and prioritize things. I suggest color-coding the cells as follows:

1) Most Critical Actions (Red)

Identify the most critical actions—the people and groups (and their respective applicable roles, barriers, and enablers) that must be addressed for the change to succeed. If you are feeling stuck, try this: do a pre-mortem. Project a year into the future (or longer, if needed). This change initiative has failed. Why? What happened to cause it to fail? If you can identify why it failed, you now have a sense of the critical aspects needed to succeed.

2) Questions and Untested Assumptions (Yellow)

Identify the areas (cells) in which there is a clear question to be answered (e.g., can we afford a consultant to act as a change agent?) or an assumption that needs to be tested (e.g., I see Martha as a potential ally, but I need to learn more).

3) Quick Wins (Green)

Identify the immediate actions you can take that are likely to be successful (e.g., Pat will almost certainly participate, based on our recent conversations). For bonus points, make note of the quick wins that will help to create the most momentum. (e.g., there is abundant evidence that our customer base is aging, but no one seems to notice. If I point it out and ask everyone to make note of it for a week, I will have a much easier time making my case for a new strategy).

TEST IT: TAKING YOUR FIRST STEPS

This final step is relatively straightforward: start taking some action and see what happens. As we mentioned in Chapter 9, it is best to focus on a handful of manageable things to start. To determine what those things should be, here are some considerations:

1. Relative Risk

Are there some potential activities that contain little to no risk? For example, can I have a frank conversation with a trusted colleague to get a better sense of the willingness to change?

2. Time Horizon

To borrow a phrase from the Special Operations teams in the military, "Slow is smooth, and smooth is fast." Where can I move slowly to develop the skills and garner support and resources for the long haul? What parts are likely to take the longest?

3. Symbolic Actions

What actions can I take that will have a lasting impact? Is there something I can do that will surprise people? When should I try it (if at all)?

With these things in mind, try to identify three concrete steps that you will begin with—and be sure to keep in mind that you are experimenting (review Chapter 9 if needed).

CONCLUDING THOUGHTS

Developing a change manifesto is a valuable exercise for creating lasting change. But, as we mentioned earlier, it can also be overwhelming. The last thing we want to see is paralysis by analysis. Remember the words of that famous philosopher, heavyweight champ Mike Tyson, "Everyone has a plan until they get punched in the mouth." This is where third-party support (for example, from a coach, a mentor, or peers outside the organization) can be so helpful. Things will not work out exactly how you anticipate, so be ready to adjust— and for crying out loud, ask for help.

14

YOU GOT THIS

"It's time for me to fly" —REO SPEEDWAGON

My friends, that's a wrap—at least for this book. But your journey is now underway, and I am so excited to see how it unfolds. Truly—this is why I get out of bed in the morning: to see leaders grow—to find, face, and embrace their Next Big Challenge (and to drink coffee). Let's take a moment to recap where we have been, and then consider what to do next.

WHERE WE'VE BEEN

Back in the introduction, I stated that this book could be summed up in three points.

1. Finding, facing, and embracing the Next Big Challenge requires hard work for leaders

2. This work is best accomplished by following the **Me1st Method**

3. This work is easier and faster with collaborative support and guidance

We began by looking at what being a Next Big Challenge leader means, and we met a few leaders who found themselves in that very spot. We looked at the three big hurdles that Next Big Challenge leaders face while recognizing that they are conquerable. We identified the seductive honeytrap of the "quick fix" approach to leadership before moving on to the science behind the **Me1st Method** solution.

Then we arrived at the main attraction: the **Me1st Method** itself. We learned about the importance of defining what we want in order to motivate ourselves and find our Next Big Challenge. We discovered the proper place of skill development and knowledge acquisition, and learned about how to assess where we are currently as we beginning facing our Next Big Challenge. We discussed how to create a strategy and begin to implement it by trying an experiment until we can embrace our Next Big Challenge. And we looked at why obtaining support is so vital in this process.

Finally, I offered some of my own support and guidance by walking you through the creation of a Personal Leadership Purpose Statement, a Team Charter, and an Organizational Change Manifesto.

WHERE YOU ARE GOING

If you are a leader hoping to **find** your Next Big Challenge, I hope this book has provided some insight, or better yet, a guide to creating your own insight as you move forward. If you are a leader **facing** your Next Big Challenge, I hope this book has shown you how to get results and make them stick. If you are a leader who needs to **embrace** your Next Big Challenge, I hope this book as given you some thoughts about what it can look like.

Regardless of the situation in which you find yourself, you are a Next Big Challenge leader.

It's your turn to grow, my friend.

I'm so glad you've given me the chance to introduce myself through the pages of this book. I'd love to tell you about the incredible community of fellow Next Big Challenge leaders who are part of the **Me1st Academy.**

If what you read here resonates with you and you decide you want more help, let's chat.

Also remember that you have complimentary bonus content available to you. Please visit:

Me1stMethod.com

LATER, GATOR...

That's it, my friends. It's been a pleasure sharing this book with you. By the way, I love to hear from my readers and listeners. If you have feedback or questions about this book, contact me through my website at Me1stMethod.com. In the meantime, I wish you all the best—and I hope to see you soon.

Keep on leading,

Mike

ACKNOWLEDGMENTS

Michelle, Gretchen, and Rachel: without our work, collaboration, and friendship, there would be no book.

The Peaceful Profits community: Mike, Deb, Jessica, Kate, Tina, Andrea and especially Mhairi: thanks for showing the way.

Laurie, Carole, Linda, and Aaron: thanks for your feedback and insights—and your friendship.

Dave, Muriel, Dorie, and the other Dave: your writing and podcasting have mentored me from afar. Likewise, Joaquín: you are always at the ready to help.

Jon, John, and Allyson—your confidence in me provided the resources for this project.

Clarissa, Kristen, and Jenna: thanks for being my reality testers.

Mom and Dad: your entrepreneurial journeys were so matter-of-fact that I almost missed them. Only now am I realizing what you accomplished.

Cate, Cora, Maryn, Eddie, and—of course—Megan: you're my world.

NOTES

3. OVERCOMING THE THREE BIG HURDLES FACED BY NEXT BIG CHALLENGE LEADERS

1. If you are involved in any creative endeavor, you must read this book.

    Pressfield, S. (2002). *The war of art: Break through the blocks and win your inner creative battles.* Black Irish Entertainment LLC.

2. Classic Brené Brown!

    Brown, B. (2021). *Atlas of the heart: Mapping meaningful connection and the language of human experience (1st ed.).* Random House.

4. THE SEDUCTIVE TRAP OF THE QUICK-FIX

1. Locke, E. A., & Latham, G. P. (2006). New directions in goal-setting theory. *Current directions in Psychological Science, 15*(5), 265-268.

5. THE SCIENCE OF LEADER DEVELOPMENT

1. The best place to begin to learn about Bowen Family Systems Theory is to visit www.thebowencenter.org . For leadership and business-focused books based on BFST, I would recommend:

    Brown, J. (2017). *Growing yourself up: How to bring your best to all of life's relationships.* Exisle Publishing.

    Fox, L.A. & Baker, K.G. (2009). *Leading a business in anxious times: A systems approach to becoming more effective in the workplace.* Care Communications Press.

2. For background on Intentional Change Theory, see:

    Boyatzis, R. E. (2006). An overview of intentional change from a complexity perspective. *Journal of Management Development, 25*(7): 607-623.

    Also see this article for theory behind all these ideas fit together:

    Taylor, S. N., Passarelli, A. M., & Van Oosten, E. B. (2019). Leadership coach effectiveness as fostering self-determined, sustained change. *The Leadership Quarterly, 30*(6).

3. Sternberg, R.J. & Detterman, D.K. (1986) *What is Intelligence? Contemporary viewpoints on its nature and definition.* Praeger.

4. Deci, E. L., & Ryan, R. M. (1985). *Intrinsic motivation and self-determination in human behavior.* New York, NY: Plenum.

6. FINDING THE NEXT BIG CHALLENGE: MOTIVATE

1. I have worked with various value clarification approaches and exercises over the years, but nothing comes close to the method that Brené Brown outlines in *Dare to Lead*.

   Brown, B. (2018). *Dare to Lead.* Vermilion.

7. FROM FINDING TO FACING THE NEXT BIG CHALLENGE: EDUCATE & EVALUATE

1. For Leader Identity research, I recommend:

   Hammond, M., Clapp-Smith, R., & Palanski, M. (2017). Beyond (just) the workplace: A theory of leader development across multiple domains. *Academy of Management Review*, 42(3), 481-498.

   Palanski, M. E., Thomas, J. S., Hammond, M. M., Lester, G. V., & Clapp-Smith, R. (2021). Being a leader and doing leadership: The cross-domain impact of family and friends on leader identity and leader behaviors at work. *Journal of Leadership & Organizational Studies*, 28(3), 273-286.

   For a useful primer on identity in organizations, see:

   Ashforth, B. E., & Schinoff, B. S. (2016). Identity under construction: How individuals come to define themselves in organizations. *Annual Review of Organizational Psychology and Organizational Behavior*, 3, 111-137.

8. A PLAN FOR FACING THE NEXT BIG CHALLENGE: STRATEGIZE

1. Locke, E. A., & Latham, G. P. (2006). New directions in goal-setting theory. *Current directions in Psychological Science*, 15(5), 265-268.

10. STRUCTURED SUPPORT FOR THE ME1ST
METHOD – AND WHY YOU NEED IT

1. One of the most useful research articles I've ever read:
   Lacerenza, C. N., Reyes, D. L., Marlow, S. L., Joseph, D. L., & Salas, E. (2017). Leadership training design, delivery, and implementation: A meta-analysis. *Journal of Applied Psychology,* 102(12), 1686.

11. CREATING YOUR PERSONAL LEADERSHIP
PURPOSE STATEMENT

1. I borrowed this idea from my friend John Sosik. I've made tweaks to it over the years but this is the source:
   Sosik, J. J., & Jung, D. (2011). Full range leadership development: Pathways for people, profit and planet. *Psychology Press.*
2. See Jack DePeters and Laszlo Bock discuss this issue at https://youtu.be/ T20XG6A9Qyw (retrieved 13 February 2022)
3. Deci, E. L., & Ryan, R. M. (1985). *Intrinsic motivation and self-determination in human behavior.* New York, NY: Plenum.

13. CREATING AN ORGANIZATIONAL CHANGE
MANIFESTO

1. This framework is presented by Mary Beth O'Neil, who cites the work of Daryl Conner.
   O'Neill, M. B. A. (2011). *Executive coaching with backbone and heart: A systems approach to engaging leaders with their challenges.* John Wiley & Sons.
2. A book about leadership and organizational life. An absolute must-read.
   Heifetz, R., & Linsky, M. (2017). *Leadership on the line: Staying alive through the dangers of change.* Harvard Business Press.

ABOUT THE AUTHOR

Mike Palanski has always been fascinated with leadership. As a boy, he and his grandfather made an annual summer trip to visit Civil War battlefields. Along the way, they'd discuss the leadership styles and tactics of the various generals. They would always look for stories about the unsung heroes, and he learned that good leadership can come from anyone.

After working in retail product management and banking, Mike obtained his Ph.D. in Leadership/Organizational Behavior from Binghamton University. His initial research focused on leader integrity, but he later transitioned to a focus on leader development. He is currently a Professor of Management at the Saunders College of Business at Rochester Institute of Technology in Rochester, NY, where he teaches courses in leadership, business ethics, and cross-cultural management. He has coached hundreds of leaders in RIT's Executive MBA program and worked with students and professionals in Ireland, Croatia, Hungary, and China. Following in the footsteps of his entrepreneurial parents, in 2020 he founded his leadership development practice, MPower2Lead, because he was tired of seeing really great people spend a ton of money on crappy, pseudo-science leader development programs, and he knew he could do better.

When he is not helping leaders to develop, he is likely to be found Uber-ing his kids everywhere, binging on Netflix with his wife, on a walk while listening to a podcast, hanging out at the family cottage on Lake Ontario, or rooting for the Pittsburgh Steelers, the Pittsburgh Penguins, the Penn State Nittany Lions, and the St. Louis Cardinals.

BEFORE YOU GO...

REMEMBER TO GET YOUR FREE BONUSES

60-PAGE COMPANION *WORKBOOK*

● ● ●

VIDEO COURSE FOR CREATING YOUR *PERSONAL LEADERSHIP PURPOSE STATEMENT*

VISIT

ME1STMETHOD.COM

www.ingramcontent.com/pod-product-compliance
Lightning Source LLC
Chambersburg PA
CBHW071123280326
41935CB00010B/1099